Instructor's Manual

The Essay Connection
Readings for Writers

Instructor's Manual

The Essay Connection
Readings for Writers

Lynn Z. Bloom

Anne M. Bowman
J. Reynolds Kinzey
Virginia Commonwealth University

D.C. Heath and Company
Lexington, Massachusetts   Toronto

Copyright © 1984 by D. C. Heath and Company

All rights reserved. No part of this publication may be reproduced or transmitted in any form or by any means, electronic or mechanical, including photocopy, recording, or any information storage or retrieval system, without permission in writing from the publisher.

Published simultaneously in Canada.

Printed in the United States of America.

International Standard Book Number: 0-669-07049-1

The Essay Connection: Readings for Writers

RHETORICAL TABLE OF CONTENTS

(page numbers refer to pages in the instructor's manual)

I. WRITING ABOUT YOURSELF AND OTHERS
1. Discovering Yourself and Others

Joan Didion, "On Keeping a Notebook"	1
Woody Allen, "Selections from the Allen Notebooks"	2
Peter Elbow, "Freewriting"	4
Studs Terkel, "John Fuller, Mail Carrier"	6
John Leonard, "The Only Child"	7

II. DETERMINING IDEAS IN A SEQUENCE
2. Narration

E.B. White, "Once More to the Lake"	10
George Orwell, "Shooting an Elephant"	12
Frederick Douglass, "Resurrection"	14
Natalie Crouter, "Release from Captivity"	16
Student Essay, Tim Payne, "Bar Harbor, Maine"	17

3. Process Analysis

How to Cook Pasta	20
Irma S. Rombauer, from "The Joy of Cooking"	
Claudia Roden, from "A Book of Middle Eastern Food"	
Elizabeth David, from "A Book of Mediterranean Food"	
Marcella Hazen, from "The Classic Italian Cookbook"	
Berton Roueche, "The Neutral Spirit: A Portrait of Alcohol"	21
Rachel Carson, "The Grey Beginnings"	24
Student Essay, Ann Upperco, "Learning to Drive"	27

4. Cause and Effect

 Sheila Tobias, "Who's Afraid of Math, and Why"   30
 Lewis Thomas, "On Magic and Medicine"   32
 Robert Jastrow, "Man of Wisdom"   34
 Student Essay, Jennifer McBride, "Rock Fantasy"   36

III. CLARIFYING IDEAS

5. Description

 Mark Twain, "Uncle John's Farm"   39
 John McPhee, "The Pine Barrens"   41
 N. Scott Momaday, "A Kiowa Grandmother"   43
 Annie Dillard, "Transfiguration"   45
 Student Essay, Kristin King, "Ontonagon"   47

6. Definition

 Ralph Ellison, "Hidden Name and Complex Fate"   50
 Bill Bradley, "Fame and Self-Identity"   52
 Judy Syfers, "I Want a Wife"   54
 Hans C. von Baeyer, "The Wonder of Gravity"   55
 Student Essay, Laird Bloom, "The Progressives' Pilgrim"   58

7. Division and Classification

 James Thurber, "University Days"   61
 Linda Flower, "Writing for an Audience"   63
 Lewis Thomas, "The Technology of Medicine"   66
 Robert Brustein, "Reflections on Horror Movies"   68

8. Illustration and Example

 Joan Didion, "Marrying Absurd"   71
 Loren Eiseley, "The Brown Wasps"   73
 Minoru Yamasaki, "The Aesthetics and Practice of Architecture"   75
 Carl Sagan, "The Cosmic Calendar"   77
 Student Essay, Lai Man Lee, "My Bracelet"   79

9. Comparison and Contrast

    Barry Lopez, "My Horse"   81
    Bruce Catton, "Grant and Lee"   83
    Suzanne Britt Jordan, "That Lean and
        Hungry Look"   85
    James Agee, "Comedy's Greatest Era"   87

IV. ARGUING: DIRECTLY AND INDIRECTLY
10. Appeal to Reason: Deductive and Inductive Arguments

    Thomas Jefferson, "The Declaration of
        Independence"   91
    Martin Luther King, Jr., "Letter from
        Birmingham Jail"   93
    Frances FitzGerald, "Ethnic Bias in
        Textbooks"   96
    Andrew Hacker, "E.R.A.--R.I.P."   99

11. Appeal to Emotions and Ethics

    George Orwell, "Marrakech"   102
    Jonathan Swift, "A Modest Proposal"   104
    Max Shulman, "Love Is a Fallacy"   107
    Richard Rodriguez, "None of This Is
        Fair"   110

V. REVISING AND EDITING
12. Revision

    Donald Murray, "The Maker's Eye: Revising
        Your Own Manuscripts" (multiple
        drafts)   113
    Linda Peterson, "Richard Wright Composes
        His Thoughts on *Black Boy*"   115
    William Zinsser, "Style"   118
    Student Paper, Draft and Revision, Angela
        Bowman, "Freddie the Fox and My Fifth
        Christmas"   121

DISCOVERING YOURSELF AND OTHERS

JOAN DIDION, "On Keeping a Notebook" (pp. 4-13)

Content

1. Didion's notebook is a collection of scenes she has observed, dialogues she has overheard, events that have gone on around her. Unlike people who keep diaries, Didion is not interested in a factual account of day-to-day activities (par. 6), but in recording the scraps of events that will help her to recall "how it felt to me" (par. 8).

2. Didion's primary purpose is "to keep in touch" with the different people she has known and events she has experienced so that she can better understand herself and her world. She wants to remember "how it felt to me." Of course, as she points out in paragraph 8, her notebook also provides material for her writing—characters, events, quotations, descriptions, details of sight, sound, setting.

3. If a writer intends to keep a notebook to himself or herself, it doesn't have to make sense to anyone else. Perhaps interpretations would be helpful to outside readers, but Didion's entries are not interpretations. They are concrete reminders that focus her memory and provide a stimulus for thinking and writing.

Strategies/Structures

1. One keeps a writer's notebook for oneself.

2. Didion is writing "On Keeping a Notebook" for us, the general public. Since Didion in fact keeps her notebook for herself, the audience for this is essay is different. Didion does not simply give us the entries from her notebook; she explains and interprets them.

3. Didion projects a complex personality. She readily

admits her weaknesses and fears. Yet she also gives herself away in paragraph 11; she is interested in "the implacable I." She is self-absorbed, witty, intelligent, a bit of a snob. Some students don't like her. As one put it, "she is criticizing the world from her Jacuzzi." Others not only like her but feel almost protective of her, as she admits her frailties and vulnerabilities.

Language

1. A conceit is a sophisticated, ingenious comparison that involves a reader's intellect; a series of pensées would be a collection of articulately stated personal observations, sometimes in maxim form. Both are intended to dazzle readers by their brilliance and wit, if not profundity. Didion's notebook does not have the formal structure of either of these literary forms, and, unlike them, it is intended for the writer, not the reader. Didion does not have to impress herself in her notebook.

WOODY ALLEN, "Selections from the Allen Notebooks" (pp. 13-18)

Content

1. Allen talks about life and death, love and loneliness, his family, and the meaning of life—and ideas for stories. All of the themes except the last are common to keepers of notebooks, and the last is certainly common for authors who keep notebooks.

2. A diary is written for one's self, so a focus on self is natural. However, since notebooks often contain the writer's musings on the universal topics mentioned above, we read them to see what others have thought about life. Although Allen's jokes do contain serious insights, they are probably most valuable as parody: they laugh us out of the self-absorption that keeping a notebook can produce.

Strategies/Structures

1. Allen parodies the concern for health that William Byrd and others display in their diaries; the sense of despair found in many modern notebooks, the use of an initial for a lover's name which Ellen Glasgow and others have done; and the ideas for plots and characters found in writers' notebooks.

2. It is probably not necessary for readers of Allen's parody to recognize his allusions in order to enjoy it. The idea of beavers taking over Carnegie Hall is funny whether the reader knows <u>Wozzeck</u> or not; the joke on "the thing with feathers" is funny whether the reader knowns Emily Dickinson or not, and so on.

3. Allen's humor works on several levels. Much of it depends on the incongruity between a supposedly profound thought ("Why does man kill?") and an illogical or absurd sequel to it ("He kills for food...and...a beverage.") He's not above being silly, but he also makes sophisticated in-jokes about modern culture. Readers might also suspect that Allen is right in suggesting that the despair of modern intellectuals is funny because it is largely self-interested.

4. The neurotic, apprehensive, and intellectual personae of Allen's movie character and his notebook are similar; the alternation between mock-seriousness and silliness is similar; the alternation between sophisticated parody and obscurity is similar.

5. The arrangement of the notebook entries is random, but the repetition of themes allows the humor to build, and the continuing saga of Allen's relationship with W., referred to intermittently, gives the piece something of a sense of plot.

6. "The Notebook" does not take itself too seriously; it's hard to make fun of someone who is already laughing at himself. It's particularly hard to parody a parody, since this mode depends on exaggerations, absurdities, and extremes.

Language

1. Allen's idea for a short story (a parody of Kafka) illustrates his mixture of dictions: the man "awakens" (elevated diction; not "wakes up") and finds himself "transformed" (almost mythical; not "changed") into lowly "arch supports." Later in the same entry "quintessence," a very formal word, is followed by "sexuality," which could be formal if it were not discovered in "bacon," a very everyday word (notice also that the soft sounds of "quintessence" and "sexuality" are contrasted to the aspiration in "bacon"). The principle of humor here is classic Allen: surprise and incongruity.

2. Consumption--tuberculosis--is a potentially dangerous disease, usually associated with dying, genteel Romantic heroines in flowing gowns. Asthma is not usually fatal and is associated with high-strung children and nervous modern intellectuals. The coupling of the two is funny; it's absurd to imagine a Romantic heroine having an asthma attack or neurotic Woody Allen behaving in a genteel, languorous manner.

PETER ELBOW, "Freewriting" (pp. 18-22)

Content

1. Freewriting is continuous, almost automatic writing which is done without concern for mechanics, clarity, style or even making sense. If a writer gets stuck, she can simply write, "I'm stuck, stuck, stuck" until she thinks of something else to write.

2. In speaking, we're confronted by a listener, so we have to come out with something, even if it's not as perfectly formed as we'd like. In writing, we're alone, so we have the opportunity to take as much time as we'd like to form our words perfectly. That opportunity presents dangers.

3. Elbow's basic point is that we can't produce ideas in writing while we're worrying about how our words

will sound to others. We're trying to do two
things at once, and our anxiety forces us to choke
off ideas before we get them down. This is
probably true, although there are other reasons why
people don't write well. Students, for instance,
often feel forced to write when they don't see any
purpose in the writing assignment. People who are
fearful of having their writing judged may find
their writing inhibited. People who don't allow
themselves enough time to plan their writing, to
write thoughtfully, or to rewrite deny themselves
the opportunity to do their best.

4. For Elbow, "voice" is the natural way each of us
has of expressing ourself; it's what comes easiest.
It we don't like our natural voices we can change
them, but we must begin by recognizing that they
exist.

5. Just plow through introductory sentences and
paragraphs; don't worry about how they sound until
after you've written the body. Then you can go
back and rewrite.

Strategies/Structures

1. It certainly seems uninhibited. It seems less
coherent than many freewritings.

2. Elbow intends this essay for people who want to
write but have mental blocks. They lack
self-confidence, so Elbow reassures them that "the
easiest thing to do is to put down whatever is in
your mind" (par. 1).

3. Freewriting can't be effective if the writer is
worrying about how it will sound to someone else.
It has to be cast off without expectation of
return.

Language

1. Elbow's tone is reassuring, but it is also
authoritative. He uses a high percentage of
imperatives and short sentences; he doesn't consider
alternatives; he makes pronouncements. This
authoritative stance does not necessarily conflict

with his attempt to reassure his audience. After all, his audience wants to write, but they need a push down the hill. They won't accept the push unless the instructor confidently assumes he can teach them how to ski.

2. Elbow avoids getting bogged down in an attempt to distinguish "editing" from "revising," "rewriting," or "proofreading." These distinctions are probably not important for Elbow's audience--people who see editing generally as whatever you do "to make your writing right."

STUDS TERKEL, "John Fuller, Mail Carrier"   (pp. 23-28)

Content

1. At 5:30 he sorts mail. Then he delivers: in a commercial area, he can walk ten miles a day and spend hours in elevators; in a residential area, he can walk twenty-five miles a day and get chased by dogs. The job ends around 2:00; many carriers go on to second or third jobs. For Fuller, the highlight is meeting people.

2. His main concerns seem to be making ends meet, taking care of his feet, and lasting until retirement. He's pleased to work in his "chosen profession." Fuller thinks of himself as a typical mail carrier.

3. The hazards dogs represent to mailmen are so proverbial that readers expect to hear about them. They are also so proverbial--the stuff of comic strips--that readers might not take the dangers seriously enough. By devoting time to them, Terkel shows them to be real dangers.

Strategies/Structures

1. The first part of the essay is arranged as a discussion of the financial needs of mail carriers. Fuller then switches to a chronological account of a

day in the life of a carrier of commercial mail, followed by an alternative day in the life of a carrier in a residential area. Then he returns to the chronological account of his own day, after work. Next, he tells some anecdotes about dogs. Finally, he returns to a chronology of his life from childhood to retirement. So, what first appears to be a straightforward account is really a fairly sophisitcated, complex arrangement.

2. This complex arrangement could have been the natural product of Fuller's conversation, but it's more likely the product of Terkel's editing. One of the paradoxes of writing is that what seems to be natural, straightforward, and relaxed is generally the product of hard work--thoughtful organization, revising, and editing.

Language

1. Direct quotation enhances the realism: this is the real language of a real working class person. Also, the easy-going, ungrammatical conversation emphasizes Fuller's easy-going, almost boyish good nature.

JOHN LEONARD, "The Only Child" (pp. 28-32)

Content

1. For most of the essay, the title seems to refer to Leonard's brother; he is an aging "flower child," and his behavior is childish, selfish, and spoiled, as that of an only child might be. At the end, Leonard twists the phrase and claims that he has become an only child, indicating that his brother is figuratively dead to the world or has literally "set himself on fire." On one hand, this culminates one theme of the essay: the brother is killing himself. On the other hand, the twist makes us realize that not only the title but the entire essay has dealt not only with the brother but with Leonard's own sense of discontent and loss.

2. California, for Leonard, is fake. Everyone becomes "an advertiser of himself." The Taco Bells and Spanish houses are fake. Leonard can only pretend to fit in; he is posing as much as his brother.

3. The brother thinks his filthy room shows his contempt for a foolish middle-class concern for cleanliness. Leonard sees this as a product of his brother's deterioration and degeneration.

4. Leonard is angry at the counter-culture because of what it did to his brother. His sarcasm in paragraph 11 is obvious.

5. Perhaps not--although many younger people do know what happened in the '60's. Leonard probably should have provided more explanation if his intended audience is made up of those people who didn't live through the '60's. However, if his real targets are Timothy Leary, R. D. Laing, and ex-counter-culture people, no more explanation is necessary.

Strategies/Structures

1. By presenting his brother's symptoms gradually, Leonard allows us to develop a more complicated emotional response to him. If we were told immediately that he was schizophrenic, we could simply pity him and write him off as bizarre. Leonard's "diagnosis" is "convincing" precisely because it is vague. Is schizophrenia an emotional problem stemming from a person's inability to relate to an environment he perceives as hostile, or is schizophrenia simply a chemical imbalance? It depends on whether you listen to R. D. Laing or to some other psychiatrist.

2. Playing varsity basketball in high school--and particularly college--indicates that Leonard's brother could have been a success according to mainstream American values. His grinning would normally indicate a happy outgoing personality, but, since the shabby coat seems to indicate that he has become almost a bum, we might back-track and consider the grinning a cover-up for his lack of ease, his embarrassment. His abilities at chess

again indicate that he could have been a success
not only because of his athletic skill but because
of his intellectual powers; however, his present
lack of concentration shows that he has wasted his
talents, his potential.

3. The problem with Leonard's brother is that finally
he is no more at ease in his own chosen context--a
filthy room--than he is in the house where
Leonard--a visiting New Yorker--is staying and
"pretends to be a Californian." The difference
between the two is that Leonard's pretense allows
him to fit into a comfortable environment; his
brother's alienation and dramatic posing will
ultimately be suicidal.

4. Leonard is angry at his brother for leaving
him--for dropping out of their old middle-class
world into a third-rate, chemically-induced
"enlightenment." He invites the reader to share
his anger, but he admits the attitude is not
charitable: "One had been pretending to be a
brother" (par. 12).

Language

1. Leonard is distancing himself from the situation
because he is raising questions that are still too
painful to address directly.

2. By not giving him a name, Leonard makes his brother
a counter-culture Everyman. He could be anyone's
brother. The blood relationship isn't
unequivocally clear until the last paragraph.

NARRATION

E. B. WHITE, "Once More to the Lake" (pp. 39-47)

Content

1. It is hard to characterize White's son, since he is generally described as White's shadow. He shadows White's present actions or re-lives his past ones. His identity is that of a "son," an almost archetypal American boy who swims, boats, fishes, and is in harmony with nature, his universe, and his father.

2. The boy fishes with his father and, as his father had done as a boy, he takes the boat out alone in the early morning. They seem to relate to the lake, the woods, the country store, and to the natural setting in much the same way. White's son also seems to allow his father the same authority as White allowed his own father. But time does pass and things do change: the modern boy wants to achieve "the singlehanded mastery" of an outboard motor; he doesn't want White's old inboard.

3. There are mornings of fishing, attended by dragonflies, afternoons of swimming, and dinners at the farmhouse with either blueberry or apple pie for dessert. In White's past, there had been the almost ritualistic packing and unpacking of trunks; there are still evenings with soda pop, streams to explore, turtles to slide off sunny logs, and tame bass to feed. There is still the comedian who wades into the water with an umbrella during a rainstorm.

4. The ending is a sharp reversal, but no one should really be surprised. The picture White has painted is literally too good to be true. Time always passes. As Hamlet's mother could have pointed out, E. B. White lost his own father, and so will White's son.

Strategies/Structures

1. After his introduction, White has a paragraph on fishing (5), one which ends with swimming (6), and one about hiking and eating (7). These simple, physical activities have not changed very much over time. However, as White moves away from nature towards more social activities, he is forced to realize that people change (end of par. 7). The next two paragraphs are given over completely to nostalgia, and by paragraph 10 he is openly contrasting the past and the present (inboards vs. outboards). The thunderstorm is last because it symbolizes nature's power to destroy.

2. The repetition is incantatory--by returning to the same words, White tries to trick us into believing that time has returned, along with the same events. There are the same early morning boatings, the same fishing, the same dragonflies, the same swimmers, the same choices of pie, etc.

3. According to Mircea Eliade, the "sacred" is an ordinary natural object which has been elevated to sacredness by our perception of its significance. The lake is sacred or holy to White because he sees it as a place where the laws of nature are suspended: time stands still. The lake and its surroundings are as quiet and, to him, as holy as a cathedral.

Language

1. From the very first sentence, there is a lack of concern for precise dates: the first summer was "along about"; the last trip was "a few weeks ago." The essay is reflective: White is constantly tagging sentences with "I wonder if...," "I remembered...," "it seemed that...," etc. The diction is informal--White uses contractions--and the pace is very slow. Details are often included not for their informational value but for their contribution to tone.

2. White certainly uses more modifiers than, for example, George Orwell in "Shooting an Elephant." He often uses adverbs to modify adjectives: "quite heavily wooded" and "infinitely remote and

primeval" (par. 3), and "utterly enchanted sea" (par. 6). In some sentences he is intentionally over-writing: "Summertime, oh summertime, pattern of life indelible, the fade-proof lake, the woods unshatterable, the pasture with the sweetfern and the juniper forever and ever, summer without end" (par. 8). White's purpose is different from Orwell's; he is intentionally setting up a feeling of idyllic lyricism that he will shatter in the last line. However, White is also perfectly capable of sparse writing: "My son, who had never had any fresh water up his nose...." (par. 2).

GEORGE ORWELL, "Shooting an Elephant" (pp. 47-56)

Content

1. Orwell's thesis is that imperialism is destructive not only for the oppressed but also for the oppressor. He makes this point generally at the beginning of paragraph 2. In this paragraph he also shows how the Burmese were oppressed, and in paragraph 7 he shows how an oppressor has lost his own freedom--"When the white man turns tyrant it is his own freedom he destroys."

2. Although our sympathy for Orwell the police officer might be limited by our own dislike for imperialism, he claims our sympathy in two ways: he admits that imperialism is wrong and he says he wants out; he also tells us he was hated--and perhaps abused--"by large numbers of people." As a lackey of the colonial state, he, too, suffers from imperialism. Orwell the narrator is older and presumably wiser than Orwell the police officer--not because his opinion of imperialism has changed, but because, we have the impression, he would now act on his opinions, rather than let the crowd bully him into committing an abhorrent act.

3. As colonial subjects, Burmese are not individuals with names or human dignity; they are seen by the English as part of the masses of humanity. The equivalent could happen in any colonial country.

4. Orwell knows that rather than killing the elephant he should simply have watched it to make sure that

it did no more damage. He betrays his convictions because he does not want to be laughed at by the Burmese. Orwell was probably more analytic when he was away from the situation, but the most damning aspect of his behavior was that he went ahead and shot the elephant anyway, even though he knew at the time that he was doing wrong.

Strategies/Structures

1. The elephant is a working animal, so it is literally "a huge and costly piece of machinery." Since the elephant is an Oriental animal and it is killed by a representative of white imperialism, the elephant could symbolize Burmese freedom. On exactly the other hand, since Orwell has already told us that the Empire is dying and has indicated that he wouldn't mind helping it to die, in killing the elephant to please the colonials, Orwell could be symbolically killing the Empire. This irony—that the murdered elephant could symbolize either the oppressor or the oppressed—is perfectly consistent with Orwell's thesis.

2. The immensely old is vulnerable, and we feel sympathy for the vulnerable. Rocks toppling and trees falling are appropriate symbols of death.

3. Orwell is more interested in demonstrating the mechanics of imperialism than in stating the conclusion that imperialism is wrong. It is appropriate, then, that he spends more time on the "mechanics," the preparation, than on the actual act and its consequences.

Language

1. Orwell's fairly simple language reflects his point that the mechanics of imperialism—despite the complexity of its consequences—are fairly simple and straightforward. The simple language also contributes to Orwell's characteristic understatement—but see Question 2.

2. The vivid language is an attempt to force home emotionally the realities of death and

suffering--realities that are generally covered over by complicated and euphemistic political rhetoric. (In the Vietnam War, "protective reaction strike" meant fire-bombing civilians in the villages.)

FREDERICK DOUGLASS, "Resurrection" (pp. 57-63)

Content

1. From that point on, Douglass was at least free in spirit; he knew that he would never submit to another whipping. He certainly could have formed this resolve at that time, although the passage of time would be required to prove the resolution.

2. Douglass does not directly call for action here, but it is significant that his narrative advocates violent resistance to slavery. Douglass would not ask, as Harriet Beecher Stowe did, only for prayers, although at times he gave abolitionist lectures under her sponsorship.

3. The root has considerable symbolic importance; it represents his relationship with Sandy and the strength of the black community. The root is symbolic of Douglass's "roots" in that community.

4. It was common in the slave community to apply Biblical imagery to the struggle for freedom. Harriet Tubman (often called "Moses") used to signal slaves to run away to the underground railroad by singing the spiritual "Steal Away to Jesus." Douglass is also directly appealing to the Christianity of his audience.

Strategies/Structures

1. Douglass focuses on his suffering, his dreadful appearance, the cold reception from his master and the contrasting warm reception from Sandy, and his final fight with Mr. Covey. Not only are these the most important incidents, they are the ones which evoke the greatest sympathy for the slaves.

2. Normally, we would divide the paragraph into

smaller units, since the organization is chronological and we seem to have several distinct events: Douglass's sickness, his beating, his return to St. Michael's, his conversation with Sandy, and the final fight. By crowding all these events into one paragraph, however, Douglass is stressing the fact that all of them are related: taken all together, they lead to one effect, which is his "resurrection."

3. Douglass elaborates on his physical appearance because it should have evoked sympathy from even the hardest of hearts. Describing Covey or Master Thomas would serve no purpose and would weaken the focus of the narrative.

4. Slave owners would probably not have read this because they already had their own view of slavery and did not want it challenged. If Douglass had been writing for blacks, he probably would have been more militant, although few blacks at the time were literate, and fewer still would have had access to his book. If he had been writing for Southern whites, he might have been more conciliatory, perhaps commenting that not all slave owners were as bad as Covey, but perhaps stressing their Christian obligations.

Language

1. Douglass's diction is fairly sophisticated. In paragraph 1 he has "intimated" instead of "said," and he was "engaged in fanning wheat" at one point. This elevated diction may at first seem inappropriate for a narrative about farm work and fighting.

2. Nevertheless, this elevated language serves Douglass's purpose by demonstrating that slaves are quite capable of becoming sophisticated, urbane people—if they're not kept busy fanning wheat in the hot sun all day. It should be noted that Douglass's autobiography underwent four major revisions during as many decades. In each successive version, as Douglass became first a national spokesman for abolition, and later a respected community citizen and Consul to Haiti for a brief time, he took pains to make the revisions

conform in content and in diction to his increasingly dignified image as a respected black spokesman.

NATALIE CROUTER, "Release from Captivity" (pp. 64-75)

Content

1. Crouter is interested in recording what happened to her and her family; she is writing a personal narrative, not recording history, and this accurately reflects her perspective. The narrow focus also gives us the feeling of being there; we can identify with these few individuals more than we could with entire armies.

2. Since Crouter intends her diary to be read by others, her entries must be fuller than those of Didion's journal. (Didion can rely on her own memory to pull together the scene; Crouter's readers obviously cannot.) Crouter gives enough explanation and details for us to understand the situation.

3. Crouter is compassionate; she seems to be concerned about individual Japanese soldiers as well as Americans. She is also curious, high-spirited and impetuous; in paragraph 11 she says she doesn't care if she gets killed; she's going to see everything. She indulges this same spirit in her son (par. 34), to whom she seems devoted. Despite her compassion for individual Japanese soldiers, she is patriotic; she joins in the singing of patriotic songs (par. 17), and she celebrates the various American accents (par. 22).

4. When people are truly hungry, food is their principal concern. By the end of the war, after four years of imprisonment, the Crouters were on the verge of starvation, and suffered the effects of many nutritional deficiencies.

Strategies/Structures

1. Crouter manages to get everything down, she has a complete account, and there's no danger of

forgetting it. The disadvantage is that readers might get swept away in the flood of details; they might not be able to distinguish what is most important or what the main point is, and they could get bored.

Language

1. This is a matter of taste, but it could be pointed out that an attempt to be figurative can sometimes weaken an essay. The hazy smoke from forest fires does cause the sun to look eerie, like a copper disc (par. 8); the description seems apt and vivid. The "rush of waves" imagery (par. 25) seems overwritten, but it does represent the stylistic experimentation of an amateur writer.

TIM PAYNE, "On the Beach at Bar Harbor" (pp. 75-79)

Content

1. Payne's state of depression is central to the essay. If he were not depressed, he would not be looking for something to change his mood; he would not be trying to "force some uplifting significance out of the beach." He becomes less depressed during the course of the essay. He is still afraid at the end, but he seems more resolved.

2. Payne expects the beach to work magically on him. He doesn't expect to have to put forward any effort.

3. The indifference of the beach forces Payne to work at the vacation. It becomes a fight, so he becomes "pugnacious." He learns that life doesn't play for you, either; you have to work at it. In the end, he has still not completely come to terms with this; he feels insignificant, like a fish which is too small (par. 5) in the hand of "something" (par. 8).

4. Payne would consider this a good vacation because he is a person who values "significance." Since significance can often be found only through

effort, for Payne, a vacation can be good even if it is not enjoyable and requires considerable effort.

Strategies/Structures

1. Payne throws these shells back because they are natural objects and should remain part of their natural setting, instead of being wrenched from their context. Payne has learned to respect the integrity of that context and doesn't want to violate it.

2. Houses are often images of the human mind. Payne interprets this house as being like his own mind--pressing against the sea and ready, bracing for some assault. He places the house at the end of the essay because it is only at the end that his mind is so prepared. Moreover, a house is a symbol of civilization, to which Payne must return.

3. Dan is not discussed because he is not of much importance, except that his occasional presence emphasizes Payne's aloneness.

4. Payne feels a sense of foreboding, objectified by the boulders (par. 4). He feels depressed, objectified by the cold (par. 5); he feels insignificant, like the shells he throws into the sea; finally, he feels "braced," objectified by the house.

Language

1. Payne is depressed, like Holden Caulfield, and he hopes to ease his depression by immersing himself in nature, as Thoreau did.

2. Nature is not always as pleasant as Thoreau would have us think; oysters remind Payne of bruises, and sea plants remind him of vomit because of their color and shape. Nature--and our natural bodies--bruise, decay, and vomit. These aspects of nature are as much a part of life as are the more aesthetically pleasing aspects, and Payne learns to accept them matter-of-factly, without disgust.

3. The images Payne evokes are of things almost immeasurably huge and frightening: the glaciers which he implies might return (par. 4) and the invisible "giant" which holds him in the end (par. 8). He is afraid of those vast forces of life and death which we cannot control. Yet he respects them (symbolized by throwing back the shells) and their integrity.

4. Payne's tone is that of a frightened person trying to come to terms with his fear. He's no coward, because a coward runs instead of trying to overcome his fear. In the end, he is neither a coward nor an overly strong person. Yet he is resolved to face whatever must be faced; this itself is a form of maturity and a manifestation of newly-realized strength.

PROCESS ANALYSIS

"How to Cook Pasta"   (pp. 85-90)

Content

1. The pasta must be put in a large pot filled with a great deal of rapidly-boiling, slightly salted water. All the pasta must be submerged, intact, and cooked until the water returns to a boil. All the writers caution against overcooking. Cooked pasta is drained and placed in a warm, lightly-greased bowl and served with grated cheese, butter, or sauce, according to individual authors' tastes. The extra information provided in each recipe lets readers know what is usually done incorrectly and shows the authors' fondness for the dish when it's prepared authentically.

2. Inexperienced cooks could consult a dictionary to determine the meaning of al dente. To determine the meanings of the other words when applied to making pasta, they could make an educated guess, based on their previous experiences in eating spaghetti and their own culinary preferences.

3. The basic instructions are the same in all the recipes. The obvious differences spring from omission of certain details and from each writer's preference for what to do once the pasta has been boiled.

Strategies/Structures

1. A directional process analysis such as a recipe is intended to be duplicated by the reader who chooses to do so. Arranging the information in any other way would be illogical, and the reader would find it difficult to follow the process--perhaps doubly difficult in light of the expectation of finding the information in step-by-step sequence.

2. Roden's directions are the briefest, with the least amount of explanation; she evidently assumes her readers are experienced cooks for whom abbreviated directions are both intelligible and sufficient. Hazan, on the other hand, is concerned with correcting misinformation, as well as with providing complete and accurate directions, for novices as well as for experienced cooks who may have been cooking pasta incorrectly for years. Thus Hazan explains her terms completely, offers translations where needed, and forewarns the reader/cook that this may taste a bit different from usual American pasta, which tends to be overcooked.

3. Hazan's directions are most interesting because of their completeness and because of the personal comments that reflect the author's personality and attitude toward the subject. We share in this writer's enthusiasm. Least interesting is Roden's brief, impersonal, objective recipe.

Language

1. Definitions are provided in the text.

2. Marcella Hazan's seems most enthusiastic (par. 5--"Soft pasta is no more fit to eat than a limp and soggy slice of bread"; par. 6--"It is therefore well worth learning how to turn it out at its best"; par. 7--"Once you have learned to cook and eat pasta *al dente*, you'll accept it no other way.").

BERTON ROUECHÉ, "The Neutral Spirit: A Portrait of Alcohol" (pp. 91-97)

Content

1. Rouèché explains that drunkenness occurs because of the way the body handles alcohol compared to other foods. While the small intestine absorbs most food, the stomach, rectum, and lungs can absorb alcohol as freely as the small intestine can. Also, the digestive acids and catalytic enzymes

necessary for digestion of food are not needed where alcohol is concerned, for it enters the bloodstream readily.

2. Roueché dispels the commonly-held belief that ethyl alcohol "is not inherently the least toxic of alcohols" by showing in paragraph 2 how it is the "least intractably toxic" because, unlike other alcohols, it oxidizes easily, is "as naturally assimilable as water," and can therefore be expelled from the body quickly. He also devotes paragraphs 4 and 5 to disproving the popular belief that a drink of alcohol has a "galvanic initial impact" because it can be absorbed directly from the stomach. This "ability of the stomach to circumspectly admit alcohol into the body," he says, is a "defensive mechanism" that protects the body "from a paralyzing inundation." In paragraph 8 he demonstrates that, contrary to the popular belief that "alcohol is absorbed most quickly in its least diluted form," alcohol diluted 10-35% is actually absorbed most quickly. These explanations seem thorough, scientifically knowledgeable, and convincing, at least to the lay reader.

3. While Roueché selects several examples that would best be appreciated by scientifically or medically trained readers, he is careful to define terms that might be unfamiliar to the average reader. For example, in paragraph 3 he explains that ethyl alcohol is the type we associate with beverages. In paragraphs 6 and 7 Roueché chooses examples from everyday life that are easy to understand--the "barroom athlete" who drinks himself to death (par. 6), the deterrent effects of food on alcohol absorption (par. 7). By giving two dramatic examples of sudden death from excessive alcohol absorption (par. 6), Roueché provides a graphic deterrent to drinking.

4. The essay would be appropriate for either audience but might be especially helpful to the novice who is unaware of what will happen physiologically when alcohol is consumed. The information might also prevent illness or death from excessive drinking through showing readers how to minimize its negative effects, as well as through its horrifying negative examples (see answer 3).

Strategies/Structures

1. Roueché begins with the inaccurate explanation to show the mythology that has long accompanied alcohol. Since his essay is a description of alcohol's progress through the body, he first needed to show how erroneous the old ideas about it were.

2. Although the common pattern has been reversed, Roueché's organization is appropriate in light of his purpose. He needs to explain the causes of the problems first, before discussing their effects and possible remedies. More than an explanation of the way alcohol travels through the body, the author's main concern seems to be explaining not only how the body but the individual can delay and perhaps prevent adverse reactions to alcohol consumption. While few readers would care to follow the examples he mentions in paragraphs 5-7, more would be interested in knowing how to avoid getting drunk. In order to understand how not to become intoxicated, readers first need to know what causes the condition. Thus Roueché begins at the beginning of the process.

3. Paragraphs 5-7 indicate that this isn't neutral, value-free writing. Nor is alcohol a "neutral" substance. When taken in excess it is harmful, even fatal. The title is ironic, as shown in the examples involving death which Roueché chooses to illustrate his discussion.

Language

1. The term "barroom athletes" indicates Roueché's scorn for those who treat drinking as a sporting event meant to determine some vague type of prowess. His example of the martini drinker clearly shows how senseless and deadly such irresponsible behavior can be. Despite the competitiveness of some drinking, it is clear from Roueché's explanation that human physiology controls alcohol absorption and its effects on the body. One cannot "train" to drink heavily without getting drunk; one can only affect the physiological reactions by altering the rate of drinking or by ingesting other

substances (such as food) along with alochol.

RACHEL CARSON, "The Grey Beginnings"   (pp. 97-109)

Content

1. Despite her speculation about this subject, Carson provides some evidence that might convince the reader of the accuracy, or at least the possibility, of her suggestions. The general reader might be convinced by Carson's own knowledge of science as she points to specific geological periods in supporting her ideas (e.g., Cambrian period in par. 22). She also establishes credibility in paragraph 2 by referring to the findings of scientists who have used the Carbon 14 method of checking matter's radioactivity to determine the age of our planet. Most convincing is her admission of the moot nature of this subject which has led to her study of that which is certain (rocks, moon, sun, and stars in par. 1). As she herself admits, this is only "a story pieced together from many sources and containing whole chapters the details of which we can only imagine" (par. 1). While such an admission might weaken the believability of her theory, it strengthens her position as an honest narrator.

    Most creationists would probably not be convinced by her evidence because there is no acknowledgment of the role of a Creator in this account. Carson relies either on scientific findings or on her own imaginative speculations rather than on Biblical texts that would contradict her position. Creationists, who rely strongly on Scriptural evidence for support of their theory, would probably disregard the findings of science because the very nature of scientific research is based on "hard," measurable, verifiable evidence. The suggestion of man's development from "inferior" life forms (par. 27) would contradict the Genesis account of the creation of Adam and Eve.

2. Readers who have had a basic course in life science at some point would be able to understand most of Carson's explanation. It is only when she refers to specific geological periods and events that the

reader might become confused. Carson has provided a built-in safeguard against future discoveries that might contradict or refute her position by explaining in the first paragraph that this is only "a story," and because there were no eyewitnesses, "there is bound to be a certain amount of disagreement" about what really happened. By establishing at the onset that her account is speculative, she avoids possible contradiction that might come from new evidence.

Strategies/Structures

1. By presenting her account in chronological order from earliest time on, Carson is able to create a sense of drama, tell an excellent story, and build up to her final and most important point: man is captivated by the sea because he is of the sea. Each paragraph adds force to this idea. The reader is constantly reminded of the time sequence by Carson's careful choice of time-related words (par. 2--"2 billion years ago"; par. 4--"the young earth"; par. 9--"days pass into months, into years, into centuries"; etc.).

2. Some scientific explanations, such as Carson's, whose intent is descriptive rather than directive ("how to") do proceed from effect to cause, in the manner of detectives analyzing evidence (effects) to yield explanations (causes). Carson's explanation, however, makes more sense in proceeding in chronological order than would the reverse, because in so doing she begins wth a simple phenomenon and establishes a sequence of progressively more complex effects, which in turn produce still greater complexities. This is far easier to understand than an explanation in reverse order would be, which would have to winnow out ever-simpler causes from a complex, intricately intertwined matrix of effects.

3. While almost every paragraph contains vivid descriptions, some are particularly forceful (par. 3--"The new earth, freshly torn from its parent sun..."). The birth metaphor is a powerful figure of speech that effectively sets the discussion of the process in motion. The ironically destructive capabilities of water are brought to life in

paragraph 10 ("From the moment the rains began to fall, the lands began to be be worn away and carried to the sea. It is an endless, inexorable process that has never stopped—the dissolving of the rocks, the leaching out of their contained minerals..."). The repetiton of key verbs ("began," "carried," "dissolved") ties in with the repetition of this part of the process. The precision of Carson's descriptions is clear because she has supplemented her scientific knowledge with imagination, and has based her speculations (the unknown) on the known.

Language

1. Although none of the terms is explicity defined in the text, the reader can assume the meanings of "congealed" (par. 5), "terrestrial" (par. 3) and "protoplasm" (par. 29) by the way Carson pairs them with more familiar terms and examples. The other words might need the clarification of dictionary definitions.

2. Several paragraphs reveal the author's respect for her subject as she refers to its many powers. In paragraph 10 she illustrates the sea's dominion in nature by describing the land's submission to the ocean's erosion process ("dissolving of the rocks, the leaching out of their contained minerals"). More important than its destructive powers, the sea also creates life (in par. 11 she explains that the sea does naturally what science can't do, and in par. 29 she asserts that we are inextricably bound to the sea by virtue of our physiological composition). Her final paragraph further illustrates her reverence for the sea as she emphasizes the role of both man and land as mere "intruders" in this "water world."

3. The author's choice of verbs serves several purposes. Each moves the narrative along quickly by showing action and change, and adds drama and suspense to a familiar subject. Some that reveal action and change are "cooling" (par. 3), "whirling" (par. 3), "changing" (par. 4), "diminished" (par. 5), "congealed" (par. 5), "sculptured" (par. 8), "shrinking" (par. 18), and "speed up" (par. 20). Others that enhance the

drama of the narration include "torn away" (par. 5), "hurled" (par. 5), "falling" (par. 9), "devouring" (par. 15), and "crumbled away" (par. 20). These verbs are particularly effective because they cause the reader to visualize the world's creation as if he had been an eyewitness.

ANN UPPERCO, "Learning to Drive" (pp. 109-114)

Content

1. Upperco isn't giving driving lessons. Her intention is to amuse the reader at her own expense and perhaps to pay homage to her father's unflagging patience as a driving teacher, and as a parent.

2. The last paragraph shows her eventual success in learning to drive. It provides a happy ending and shows that continued practice at something can yield positive results. That she not only learned to drive but liked it as well offers the reader a hopeful message about difficult endeavors: don't give up!

3. Whether or not they have ever learned to drive, all readers have had the experience of tackling some skill that involved following steps. There is a universality in Upperco's account that allows all to identify with her trials and errors. It's our recollection of our own "klutziness" that makes this funny. She does intend to ridicule herself for the sake of the essay's humor (as Thurber does in "University Days," pp. 231-238). Her close scrapes with disaster are funny because she survived them without serious consequence. These moments add humor since the danger passed in spite of her fear at each slip-up.

Strategies/Structures

1. The process of moving from non-driver to seasoned "pro" forms the organization of Upperco's essay. First she learns to maneuver the automatic Chevy, then she masters the standard transmission Pinto.

2. Upperco's ability to laugh at her mistakes makes the reader sense she's no longer a novice, even though this doesn't explicitly come out until the last paragraph. Self-ridicule oten accompanies the distance a person acquires after an embarrassing experience. We assume she's mastered the art of driving by the attacks she makes on her earlier ineptitude. A person who had never learned might not have been so openly self-critical. Because she knows how to drive, she can choose this mocking, humorous tone and not worry about the audience's laughter. She's laughing too.

3. Upperco's essay is built on comic scenes which we see by way of descriptions and exaggerations. In paragraph 2 she shows us the terror on the other driver's face ("...her eyes were as big as golfballs!"). The image continues as she talks about her life flashing before her own eyes. Her mother's white-knuckled behavior whenever the learner got behind the wheel is another example (par. 4). In paragraphs 5 and 6 she puts us in the back seat of the Pinto as she learns the thrill of shifting gears, an especially funny scene to anyone who has ever gone through this process or watched someone else do it.

Language

1. That she refers to certain driving techniques (looking through rear view mirrors, slipping the clutch) without defining them indicates she's writing for others who also know how to drive. The language choice makes the essay funny to the experienced driver but not perhaps to the novice or non-driver who belongs to the category she placed herself in and then ridiculed.

2. From the first paragraph we know this is funny by her description of the quiet neighborhood once again being demolished by the student driver. Since she's poking fun at herself, she's giving her readers the liberty to join in.

3. Each time she feels momentarily sure of herself, Upperco uses overstatement (par. 4--"Confident now of my driving prowess" and par. 5--"When I had

mastered (in a manner of speaking) the skill...") to set the reader up for her setbacks. Her understatements about her mother's nervousness also add humor (par. 4--"Mom's behavior in the front seat tended to make me a trifle nervous"). By referring to the Chevy as a "tank" and the Pinto as a "rattle trap," she not only offers descriptions of the vehicles but amuses us as well. Similarly her father's direct quotations, often understatements, allow Mr. Upperco to "come to life" for the reader. We learn a great deal about him from what he says, in addition to his forbearing behavior.

4. By combining formal and informal language, Upperco reveals the formality and casualness of this learning process. Driving is serious business, but as she clearly shows, it can, with practice, become fun.

CAUSE AND EFFECT

SHEILA TOBIAS, "Who's Afraid of Math, and Why?" (pp. 122-129)

Content

1. Tobias is convincing as she explains social and attitudinal factors that seem more logical causes of math anxiety than any physiological explanation. Answers to the rest of the question will vary.

2. When the problem became evident, people sought an explanation for the cause. Although there is no solid proof that people either are or aren't born with math aptitude, this became a convenient explanation and excuse in some cases. Some effects are the following: some students have low expectations of their ablility to do math successfully, which are reinforced by doubtful parents (par. 3 and 4). Also, with less math education, women regarded math-related professions as those dominated by men and consequently avoided entering such fields. People who didn't do well in math felt in some way mentally inferior to those who mastered it, and females who did well as others of their sex struggled felt like anomalies.

3. Tobias's biological argument seems convincing since researchers themselves have been unable to find any physiological differences between the sexes regarding math aptitude. The fact that some females do excel in math also makes this theory doubtful. The psychological argument is a bit less convincing. While isolated cases support the point that females aren't as pressured as males by peers, parents, or professionals to do well in math, many readers might argue that Tobias is generalizing here. Although past social conditioning has encouraged particular sex-role behavior, Tobias' final point seems dated and debatable.

Strategies/Structures

1. As the title implies, the essay is addressed to those who either are math anxious but don't know why or those who aren't math anxious and want to understand why others are. Knowledge of math isn't essential to understand the essay. Tobias identifies possible causes which some readers might be able to recognize quickly, but math-anxious readers won't feel "at ease" until practical advice is given that will eliminate the difficulties.

2. Tobias makes indifferent readers aware of how serious and far-reaching math anxiety is for those who are sufferers. The sufferers might take heart from the author's understanding and sympathy. Tobias' analysis of the depressing effects of math anxiety (known all too well by math casualties) may be discouraging. However, since she demonstrates that its causes are cultural rather than biological, she prepares the way for the cures she discusses later in her book, <u>Overcoming Math Anxiet</u>y, from which this is taken.

Language

1. A myth is a fictional account often aimed at explaining some phenomenon but exclusive of scientific investigation. The word is appropriate since Tobias shows there is no scientific proof to support the idea that math ability is biologically predetermined.

2. Tobias implies that a math underachiever is the student who is fearful of risk-taking and independent thought, and is equally reluctant to solve problems by using new systems not tried before. The term "feminist" is indirectly defined by the example Tobias gives of these individuals who are irritated by sex-role stereotyping of little girls. Neither term is value-free since most readers, based on their own experiences and philosophies, will react to them positively or negatively.

LEWIS THOMAS, "On Magic in Medicine"   (pp. 130-136)

Content

1. An act of magic is an attempt to manipulate a situation--conjure a demon, cast a love spell, or strike an enemy with a plague--by means of a formula or ritual that cannot be explained or demonstrated through the commonly accepted rules of science. An act of magic in medicine would be an attempt to improve one's health by means of a formula, technique, diet, or practice that cannot be explained by current scientific thought. The field is ripe for these acts of magic in medicine because people, often desperately, want to improve their health, and they often have no notion of what practices are scientifically accepted. They accept medical practices which work, or which they hope will work, without demanding to know why these practices work.

2. The explanation of a single cause is sufficient for microbial infections--diseases that are caused by the presence of a particular microorganism. More complicated diseases, such as cancer and heart disease, cannot be explained by a single cause.

3. Thomas is skeptical about the effectiveness of the "Seven Healthy Life Habits" because no one has offered a reasonable explanation of how, for example, skipping breakfast can damage a person's health. Furthermore, even in cases where some explanations are possible (health problems resulting from smoking or lack of exercise), Thomas warns that we should not go too far in our claims. Cancer is complicated--it can be caused by many factors--so the elimination of one factor does not necessarily eliminate the risk of cancer.

4. These studies begin with the "effect"--long life or premature death--and then try to reason back to the cause without offering a comprehensive, unequivocal explanation of how the cause and effect are related. The logic is not very far removed from the most superstitious: "The man died Saturday. On Friday, he had walked under a ladder. Ergo, he died because he walked under a ladder."

5. It is difficult to convince people that we can't always explain disease simply because people don't want to accept that truth. We desperately want to believe that somebody--doctors, witch-doctors, the makers of natural foods--understands disease and can tell us how to avoid it, and so we tend to put our skepticism aside when someone makes such claims. To have an answer in hand--however poorly-founded it may be--is much more comfortable than to have the lack of an answer verified by experts.

Strategies/Structures

1. It might be difficult initially to convince people that we--good modern people--believe in magic, but it's relatively easy to convince us that our ancestors did. By tracing our beliefs in magic historically, Thomas does show us that our belief in magic is very old, but, by showing how our "magic" has become more scientific, he holds out the hope of progress. The history of tuberculosis is a case in point. Once we believed in the magical powers of sunlight to ward off the disease; now we understand the biological cause and can rely on the demonstrable power of specific drugs.

2. In paragraphs 5 and 17, Thomas begins by stating an effect--which, in both cases, is a tough problem for doctors--and then tries to explain why the problem exists--what causes this problem. This reversal is sometimes awkward because it slows down the pace of our reading; instead of building to a conclusion, which can be done quickly, the writer approaches his point in a more roundabout fashion. The reversal is justified here because the problems illustrate Thomas's point: straightforward answers become complicated because of spontaneous remissions, and so, as Thomas suggests at the end of paragraphs 5 and 17, we need to admit our ignorance, keep cool heads, and take the time to figure things out.

3. Thomas is writing for a combination--or, more precisely, for those of us whose attitudes are a combination. Diehard enthusiasts won't believe Thomas; skeptics don't need his warnings. However,

those of us who are tempted to believe in
magic--but know we shouldn't--may do so.

Language

1. A "paradigm" is the example for study; he uses the
   term "edited out" because the disease has not been
   eliminated or removed but simply moved from one
   list to another; "lucky anomalies" are those few
   diseases with single causes. They are anomalies
   because they are rare, and lucky because they are
   often easily treated. "Multifactorial in nature"
   means having more than one cause, and "spontaneous
   remission" is the disappearance of a disease "on
   its own," not as a result of treatment.

2. "Bifurcated" is appropriate because it implies an
   almost schizoid state--we believe in both
   rationality and "magic." "Ideological" is accurate
   and appropriate in its connotations because it
   implies that this thinking is emotional and
   dogmatic rather than logical. "Subliminal" is
   accurate because the "7 come 11" idea is not openly
   expressed; it is appropriate to Thomas's discussion
   since "magic" belongs to the subconscious, the
   realm of the subliminal. "Doctrine" implies a
   systematic body of belief, whereas "notion"
   connotes a less substantial, more frivolous idea.

ROBERT JASTROW, "Man of Wisdom"   (pp. 136-142)

Content

1. Yes, because it begins with what is less known--the
   evolution of primitive man--and moves forward to
   what we do know, man as he is now. By moving in
   this direction, Jastrow can conclude with at least
   apparent certainty, and we, as readers, can look
   back and understand what has evolved in the essay,
   just as we, as Homo sapiens, can look back and
   understand the evolution of the race.

2. Since we are so far removed from the events Jastrow
   describes, much of his reasoning must be
   speculative. We have evidence that ice ages and

migrations took place, but we can only speculate on what caused the migrations. Similarly, we have evidence that man's brain size increased, and we have evidence that he endured cold weather, learned to make tools, and learned to speak. Whether man's activities caused the brain to grow—or whether the increased brain size made these activites possible—remains a matter for speculation. Speculation does not weaken Jastrow's argument; grounded in the evidence he has, speculation makes his argument possible.

3. Jastrow does think that there is a causal connection between the changes in climate and man's growth in brain size: people with larger brains endured the cold and passed on their genes, and people with smaller brains did not. His arguments for a "survival of the fittest" certainly seem reasonable, and again, since we cannot have any direct evidence, we are forced to settle for good reasons rather than hard facts.

Strategies/Structures

1. Jastrow's essay does not demand an elaborate understanding of "natural selection" or "survival of the fittest." He does use the term "natural selection" and cite Darwin in paragraph 12, but he has already explained the term in paragraphs 6, 7, and 8.

2. Since much of Jastrow's argument relies on speculation and reason (see Content, question 2), people could choose not to be convinced. Diehard "creationists" would probably so choose. However, Jastrow can certainly claim that he has provided a reasonable explanation of the evidence we do have (fossil evidence of the human brain's evolution, paragraph 12), and he could challenge others to provide other reasonable explanations.

3. Jastrow's existing organization is the most convincing order (see Content, question 1). Reversing the order would lead us back into uncertainty and would not seem convincing or satisfying.

Language

1. The most important thing to know about Ice Age Homo is that he lived during the ice ages; as Jastrow points out in paragraphs 6 and 7, man's entire existence was conditioned by his struggle with the cold. This struggle is central to Jastrow's argument, of course, since it was this struggle that began the evolution Jastrow describes. Homo erectus--the man who stands erect--distinguished man from the beasts by his very posture. Homo sapiens, of course, is the man of wisdom--ourselves, we hope. The essay is titled "Man of Wisdom" for two reasons. First, it is a record of how we arrived at our present stage of development. Second, the title is vocative: Jastrow is speaking to us, as people of wisdom.

2. On one hand, by using the language of myth, Jastrow tacitly admits that the theory of evolution is not an historical record, but an attempt to interpret the history of mankind. On the other hand, by echoing the language of religion, Jastrow demonstrates that scientific speculation stems from the same human need as do all religions: the need to explain who we are and how we got here.

JENNIFER McBRIDE, "The Rock Fantasy"   (pp. 142-147)

Content

1. These stars, according to McBride, have the ability to control the emotions, imaginations, and physical motions of their audiences (par. 5). Often they are accepted as heroes since they do on stage what their patrons aren't at liberty to do in their own worlds. McBride implies that the rock stars' audience is young and impressionable. By implication, the rock stars would not be so appealing to older audiences with more mature judgment, who are less easily manipulated.

2. While she explains the star's awareness of being in character during a performance, McBride feels his definition comes from each concertgoer who

imaginatively projects particular qualities onto the star, which the star may not actually possess (par. 7).

3. By being "mysterious," the star maintains distance from the audience and allows everyone's imagination to run freely (par. 4). This distance also keeps his work separate from his private life, which isn't unique to members of this profession. All of the trappings of stagecraft--lighting, costumes, makeup, music, sets--create and help sustain the illusion of "otherworldliness."

4. In paragraphs 4 and 9, McBride reminds readers that these stars are mortal and are as capable as anyone else of questionable, even poor behavior, manipulative, egocentric, sexually suggestive (par. 4). Although they flout the conventions of bourgeois society, they exaggerate these conventions in their personal greed and materialism. They are not worthy of reverence regardless of the illusion they help create.

Strategies/Structures

1. McBride isn't writing for rock fans. Her question at the end of paragraph 1 implies surprise--hers and perhaps that of readers who share her views--at those who buy concert tickets with hard-earned cash. Paragraph 2 confirms her attitude as she describes the loudness, the "aural assault," and "bad acoustics" heard at these concerts. As she herself admits, ardent concert fans aren't going to sympathize with her complaints.

2. McBride asks the same questions she assumes her readers have asked about the appeal of rock concerts. The questions reveal her attitude toward the subject and provoke agreement from those who share her views. No answers are given immediately after each question, but McBride implies the answers rest with the star's seductive powers. The reader finds the answer by reading the essay through.

Language

1. The title mirrors the author's belief that everything associated with rock concerts is of an unreal, fantastic nature. Fantasy might be interpreted as that which is unreal but temporarily accepted as real; the belief itself may be pleasurable, harmless, or destructive.

2. In paragraph 2 McBride talks about "loud" concerts, "out-of-tune guitars," "faltering" voices, and "bad acoustics." The sense of smell is affected by the "stench of beer" (par. 2) and the odor of "strange smoke" (par. 4). In paragraph 3 she describes the atmosphere of the concert hall shrouded in "eerie darkness" which is "magical, otherworldly, reminiscent of a childhood never-never land."

3. In the first sentence her references to the concert as a Mecca is a metaphor. The hall is compared to the holy site. Comparing the star to a _deus ex machina_ ("god out of the machine") is another metaphor that enhances the god image. The Dionysus metaphor in paragraph 4 also sustains the image.

DESCRIPTION

MARK TWAIN, "Uncle John's Farm" (pp. 155-162)

Content

1. The use of extensive details and words that elicit sensory and emotional responses from the reader, as well as the inclusion of such particulars as people's names and descriptions of their behavior, make Twain's account convincing and credible. This recollection indeed seems ideal, but Twain's Garden of Eden is not without its snakes—and bats and cold baths on winter mornings.

2. While the farm might have been splendid, it became even more so to Twain with the passage of time. This distance has transformed Uncle John's farm into "a heavenly place for a boy" and for an aging writer. Any unpleasantness has faded and has become lost in the wealth of fond remembrances.

Strategies/Structures

1. The catalogues remain lively and fresh because Twain doesn't appeal to just one sense as he makes his lists. Like Twain (the child) we are struck by the sight of all the comestibles spread before him, the aroma of the countless meats and sweets, the heat of home-made battercakes and breads, and the coldness of dairy products mentioned in paragraph 3. Our senses are equally engaged in paragraph 13 ("earthy smells" and "odors of wildflowers," "the sheen of rain-washed foliage," "the rattling clatter of drops" and "hammering of woodpeckers"). When one sense is stimulated by a description, Twain quickly engages another. This keeps the reader interested; the lists are anything but dull and boring.

2. Paragraph 13's details let us experience what Twain himself experienced. The richly descriptive

passages are as effective as film footage shot by a skilled photographer. As one moment intrudes upon another, our attention is directed to the things Twain---the verbal photographer---wants us to see, hear, feel, smell, and taste all at once. Breaking this paragraph into smaller units would have destroyed this total inundation and indulgence of the senses, the solidity of the sensual impact. In organization, Twain also moves from summer to winter, day to night, and outdoors to indoors; he closes with a snug interior scene, as cozy as a Dutch painting of similar subjects.

3. The long sentence in paragraph 6 is broken up by punctuation, namely semicolons and dashes, and by conjunctions ("and," "but," "for"). Twain maintains unity by using dependent clauses that depend on the paragraph's first sentence for clarity ("I can see the farm yet, with perfect clearness"), with parallel construction of phrases and clauses throughout, and through the repetition of such phrases as "I can see...." Despite the repetition of participial phrases and dependent clauses, Twain achieves variety in his choice of subjects and verbs. The aunt, uncle, cousins, and pets are all doing different things at different times. There is constant change and activity.

4. Each anecdote serves as description. Where adjectives alone might not be sufficient to convey a person's personality or behavior, a more complete description is provided by these short narratives. Thus Aunt Patsy's fear of snakes comes to life as Twain tells her reaction to finding them in her work basket; it "disordered her mind"--though Twain's tone leads us to assume this is an hyperbolic statement.

Language

1. Answers will vary, but one of the earliest examples is found in paragraph 5, where Twain recalls the joy of swimming in off-limits water holes and concludes by saying, "For we were little Christian children and had early been taught the value of forbidden fruit." Here we see both child, only concerned with having fun, and adult, capable of interpreting the irony of disobedience in light of

Christian upbringing. The adult language implies both a grownup perspective and an awareness of a child's perspective, including references to Christian children and to bats as "coleoptera" (par. 7)--wrongly, for humorous effect, since if the adult reader recognizes this technical word he probably knows that it refers to beetles, not bats.

2. The repetition has a cumulative effect of enhancing Twain's nostalgic tone and mood, and of enveloping the reader in its engaging embrace.

JOHN McPHEE, "The Pine Barrens" (pp. 163-171)

Content

1. McPhee is fascinated by the Pine Barrens. As he explaines to Brown in paragraph 11, "I was in the pines because I found it hard to believe that so much unbroken forest could still exist so near the big Eastern cities, and I wanted to see it while it was still there." McPhee is also taken with the few inhabitants who, like their surroundings, seem untouched by the progress and problems of a modern world. He seems amazed by the hospitality and generosity of Brown, who readily accepts him as a guest and makes "a considerable" offer to fix him lunch (par. 6). He also admires the concern Bill Wasovwich has for the Pine Barrens' future if an airport is built there (par. 14). While the author spends a good deal of time in the first two paragraphs revealing his attitude about the place itself, much of the essay is spend describing his interaction with the inhabitants. We can assume the fondness he feels for the people has contributed to his attitude toward the place itself.

2. National parks are easily recognizable for readers while the Pine Barrens may not be. These references serve as points of comparison. Readers who have visited or at least have knowledge of such spots as the Grand Canyon, Yosemite, and the Smokies can grasp the expansiveness of this little-known location because of McPhee's analogy.

3. Like his surroundings, Brown is relatively

untouched by a high-tech society. His needs are basic: food, shelter, companionship. He is a sturdy, unpolished, "natural" man who mirrors his environment. His home is a microcosm of the Pine Barrens. The tokens of the modern world (par. 3--"old cars," "refrigerators," "vacuum cleaners," "engine heads") dot the periphery of his home and lie in waste. His needs are satisfied inside his house. Similarly, the modern world itself is outside the door of the Pine Barrens, yet what is essential to the inhabitants remains within the wooded boundaries.

4. Bill Wasovwich is shy with strangers, and protective of his privacy. Like an animal of the woods, he has a natural homing instinct when he's on one of his 30-mile day trips (par. 5), and a symbiotic relationship with both his environment and his friend, Fred Brown, another inhabitant of the woods. At the same time he is concerned about the possible encroachment of civilization on the forest (par. 14). McPhee's description of Bill shows us the endangered species of the Barrens. Through him we are made aware of the potentially tragic consequences that progressive change might have for him and his home.

Strategies/Structures

1. The view widens beyond the 12-mile radius, and the reader sees 650,000 acres of forest. By the end of the paragraph, McPhee elevates us above the scene to a height that allows us to see the whole East Coast with the Pine Barrens as "the geographical epicenter of the developing megalopolis."

2. The narrowing of focus eventually leads to McPhee's description of Fred Brown. Despite the vastness of the setting, the essay then concentrates on one of the Pine Barrens' residents.

3. The organization is spatial, proceeding from far to near. There is consistent inward movement that takes the reader through what seems like concentric circles. Through his descriptions, McPhee takes us from wilderness to dirt path to yard to living room to kitchen--the "epicenter" of Brown's home. Details of the kitchen are first arranged

laterally—what McPhee sees at eye level from his seat—and then from bottom (rugs on the floor) to top (calendars, photos, and a framed poem on the walls).

4. Both descriptions enhance McPhee's characterization of Brown. The allusive but not graphic description of the woman on the postcard "wearing nothing at all" attests to Brown's sense of humor as well as to his virility—that at his age he can roguishly claim to have a nubile girlfriend. McPhee includes the information about the cars to let us know more about the owner. Brown values his possessions (each had "been his best car" at some point), and he keeps them even when they are no longer functional. Also, he's not a very careful driver, which perhaps reflects how unskillful he is with items from an outside, mechanized world that are introduced into his natural habitat.

Language

1. The effect is reminiscent of an echo—the kind one is likely to hear in the stillness of a forest. Even the inhabitants' speech is reflective of their natural setting. Three repetitions of the triplet, "That's God's water," are reminiscent of the Biblical style and reinforce the reverent attitude of the inhabitants (and McPhee) toward this sanctified setting.

2. The colloquial, ungrammatical quotations are vigorous and vivid punctuations to McPhee's more subdued, grammatically correct, elegant style.

N. SCOTT MOMADAY, "A Kiowa Grandmother"   (pp. 172-179)

Content

1. Momaday joins his three subjects by using his grandmother as the connecting link. Through his recollections of her we learn of the land, the Kiowa, and their culture. Although there is no explicitly stated thesis, the reader senses Momaday's sadness at the passing of so noble a race

(represented by his grandmother) and the pride he has in his heritage.

2. Momaday is writing for those unacquainted with the Kiowa, which accounts for his descriptions of their origins, beliefs, lifestyle, and historical changes. Obviously this information would be unnecessary for a Kiowa audience familiar with tribal lore.

3. In keeping with his descriptions of nature's importance to the Kiowa, Momaday includes the legend to show the tribe's spiritual beliefs. Although this theology might seem at odds with that of Christians, Momaday effectively shows the white man's religious intolerance of the Kiowa which, ironically, forced them to give up their religion.

4. Like her kinsmen, she values nature (par. 8--"reverence for the sun"), but she gives up her past tribal beliefs (par.8--"She was a Christian in her later years"). The "postures" he describes in paragraph 10 are in harmony with those of other Kiowa women who cooked, did beadwork, and prayed (in par. 10, 11).

5. Rainy Mountain is a knoll northwest of the Wichita Mountain Range in Oklahoma. Symbolically it is the resting place of the Kiowa civilization. While there might be several literal ways to get there, Momaday gives us the figurative directions: the traveler must be a Kiowa to understand the journey and his destination.

Strategies/Structures

1. The solitary little insects against the expansive natural backdrop parallel man's insignificance in the vastness of the world. Like Aho, the insects are small representations of life that survives--sometimes alone--in this desolate location.

2. Momaday's combination of close-up and distant views shows there is more to the Kiowa than what might be seen in a quick glance. He wants to make sure we're not so taken with the panorama that we overlook the fine details. His people are worth

knowing more about; they're not just part of the scenery.

3. By combining the sounds as well as the sights, Momaday shows their gregarious nature and brings them to life. We see the Kiowa both at work and at play. Some of the seeming cultural differences disappear as Momaday describes the gossiping women who make "loud and elaborate talk among themselves, full of jest and gesture, fright and false alarm" (par. 11). They enjoy singing, good food, and "a lot of laughter and surprise" (par. 11). These details enable us to see that we have more in common with the Kiowa than we may have realized. Momaday makes use of other sensory details (par. 10--the Kiowa abide the cold but are "summer people"; par. 9--Aho turns "meat in a great iron skillet"; par. 1--"steaming foliage seems almost to writhe in fire"; and the prairie's heat is like "an anvil's edge").

Language

1. Although the author doesn't speak the Kiowa language, he has observed them and learned their ways since childhood when he spent much time with his relatives (par. 10, 11). We can assume some of these relatives could communicate in both languages, since Momaday provides a translation of the Devil's Tower legend his grandmother taught him (par. 7).

ANNIE DILLARD, "Transfiguration" (pp. 180-184)

Content

1. In both settings Dillard is a keen observer of what's going on around her. She looks for details and makes analogies between what she sees in nature and what she sees in herself. In both settings she seems quiet, contemplative, and inquisitive about her role in life. She sees herself resembling the moths, and writing is the flame to which she is drawn.

2. Dillard seems to be conveying the following message: writers must be dedicated to their craft to such an extent that it becomes the all-consuming purpose for their being.

3. Serious writers value writing above all else—even when they are doing other things. They are driven by their art and must make sacrifices in order to reach their goals. Like the moths who have been consumed in flames, writers also lose some of themselves in order to become what they want to become: writers. The candles in paragraph 11 serve as reminders to Dillard of what her ultimate mission in life is. Even though friends appear and their faces are momentarily illuminated by the candles' glow, Dillard will always come back to the flame, her writing.

Strategies/Structures

1. Dillard includes all the details for an audience not used to observing very carefully what is around them. She sets herself apart from others (even aspiring writers) because of her keen eye and her desire to share these observations through her writing (par. 10—"They had no idea what I was saying").

2. Few people would take the time to notice a spider's web that rests behind a toilet (par. 2) or count the number of insect carcasses it has yielded. Dillard scrutinizes these with such care that she can even label them as "mostly sow bugs" (par. 3) or earwigs or spiders. Even in their decomposed state she can identify a thorax or abdomen or "arching strips of chitin" (par. 3).

3. Dillard equates the moth's sacrificial death to her own sacrifice as a writer. Something must be given up (i.e., life) in order for something greater to be gained. Like the moth, the writer must be a martyr of sorts—"a hollow saint" (par. 9)—hollow because the writer's core of being or essence is moved from within to the printed page. The image is extremely effective in light of her own perceptions of the writer's role in life.

4. Dillard delays in making the analogy complete until

paragraph 10 so that readers can first appreciate her perceptiveness in understanding the sacrifices that are made even by nature's smallest creature. By paragraph 10 readers realize the comparison she has made. She has allowed us to share her same observations and at this point reach the same conclusion.

Language

1. The insects are her aquaintances, perhaps friends, and each is an individual to her. She has learned something important from them and therefore uses these specific pronouns as a sign of their importance to her. Answers to the remainder of the question will vary.

2. Active verbs in paragraph 7 include the following: "burnt," "flapped," "dropped," "frazzled," "fried," "ignited," "clawed," "curled," "blackened," "jerked," and "crisped." All describe the moth's agonizing death and in turn suggest the pain Dillard herself experiences as a writer.

KRISTIN KING, "Ontonagon"   (pp. 185-187)

Content

1. Ontonagon was a mining town that sprang up to accommodate miners and their families. When the ore ran out, the town became a shell. From her description, King tells us of the town's dirt (par. 2), its few remaining businesses (par. 1), its public meeting places (par. 9), and its sand and grass-covered sidewalks (par. 10).

2. King's appearance brings the voice of authority to her description. We believe her since she's been there. She refers to herself (and perhaps a companion) as "we" while the townspeople are always "they." Also, she never indicates having any conversation with them. Without her presence, the description would lack authenticity and the intimacy she establishes with the reader through her observations.

3. The incident tells us more about Ontonagon's inhabitants, and here they speak for themselves. Their needs and tastes are basic, their conversations sparse, their hospitality nonexistent. The vignette "shows" rather than "tells" these things.

4. The town is as colorless and dull as the inhabitants. The businesses cater to the primary needs of rather unsophisticated people, and both are without joy.

Strategies/Structures

1. Visually, King tells us about the town's ugliness and filth (par. 2--"smut" on screen doors, and par. 10--"dead flies on the windowsill"). She also describes some of the residents' clothing (par. 3--"apron over sweatshirt and jeans" and a man in "thick-soled boots" and "red plaid lumber jacket," and par. 10--"women in their tight knit pants and sleeveless blouses"). Details about taste include the frozen pizza in paragraph 3, the man's ketchup-choked meal of ham and potatoes in paragraph 8, and the waitress' question about adding onions in paragraph 4. The sense of touch is stirred by the words "dirt" (par. 1), "smut" and "ice-chunked" (par. 2), and "stubbled chin" (par. 3), while smell is called into play by "paper mill" (par. 1), "'homefries ' ham'" and "'onions'" (par. 4), and "coffee" (par. 8). Sound details include ore being "blasted" (par. 1), the wind blowing snow (par. 2), the screen door that slams shut (par. 3), and coffee that is gulped (par. 8).

2. The dismalness of the town is juxtaposed with its impressive natural surroundings, and the contrast is clear. Another arrangement might have destroyed King's point: the town was grim from any angle.

3. The word "they" makes the reader wonder if King means the flies or the people. She means both. For dramatic effect, this one-sentence paragraph is appropriate. Nothing is going to change in Ontonagon.

Language

1. The pronouns emphasize her role as outsider (see Content, answer 2). By using only "we," the audience assumes those with her share her views and see things as she sees them.

2. Her tone is consistently critical, and her word choice reflects her dislike for the town (par. 1--"Ontonagon was an ugly, weather-beaten town") and its unfriendly inhabitants (par. 9--"The people in town never gave much more than a nod").

DEFINITION

RALPH ELLISON, "Hidden Name and Complex Fate" (pp. 194-200)

Content

1. To some extent, since we are all named by someone else—usually our parents—we all have to learn to live with our names. However, white people's names often stress their continuing place in the dominant culture; whites are named for Christian saints, American political or folk heroes, or relatives. Ethnic groups sometimes name their children to remind them that they are a part of that ethnic group, but the names still stress a continuing cultural identity. On the other hand, blacks, who were often given family names by slaveholders—and members of ethnic groups who were "renamed" because they couldn't speak English—carry in their names a reminder that they live in a country dominated by a white, western European culture that is at best somewhat alien and, at worst, hostile.

2. Ellison's thesis is that we must use our names to help develop a sense of self-identity. We do this by making our names—our sense of self-identity—"the center of all our associations in the world" (par. 5). It has often been difficult for blacks to create a sense of identity because the white world has always tried to impose an identity, a name, on them (slave names, the term "Negro," the hostile term "nigger," etc.).

3. People change their names to break away from their past, to deny (very rarely to restore) their ethnic heritage, to create new identities—and perhaps new chances for themselves. They may also change names in order to be identified with the dominant majority.

4. The child named after a famous person may feel pressured into living up to the name—becoming it—instead of creating his own identity and making

the name his own. This can happen to "juniors" as well.

Strategies/Structures

1. Ellison's own story is a particular example of the general statements of part one. He is like Franklin D. Roosevelt Jones, the example in the first half. If you think of him only as the writer, Ralph Waldo, you'll miss the man Ellison, which is the more important part of his identity. In paragraph 13--a very short paragraph--is the obvious transition, but notice that Ellison has already slipped into the first person singular in paragraph 9.

2. The photographic lens is almost an identity for the child. Like his own particular name, it is the one thing that he has that no one else--not even the white boys--has. It is also perhaps symbolic of the writer's way of perceiving, even though it will take some time to learn "the technique" (par. 1).

Language

1. The more formal language is appropriate for the political, historical, even "mythic" discussion of the black race in general. The less formal language of the second half is more fitting for Ellison's informal personal narrative.

2. "Negro" is a nearly clinical word; we don't call white people "Caucasian" unless we're speaking in an almost scientific context. As long as people were "Negro," they could be treated as members of a category, not as living individuals. "Negro" was the white man's term to describe something alien to himself; "black" is a name black people have made their own as they have forged their own self-identity.

BILL BRADLEY, "Fame and Self-Identity" (pp. 201-206)

Content

1. The athlete may become too cocky (par. 10); he may lose his privacy (opening anecdote); the worst danger is that he may allow others to determine his own life for him and so lose his own sense of identity.

2. Boorstin's main distinction is that a hero is remembered throughout time while a celebrity is quickly forgotten. Most of us can remember the important generals of the Civil War, but how many of us can name the quarterbacks of the Super Bowl teams of five years ago?

3. Self-definition is the individual's own understanding of himself or herself. It is valuable because other people come and go but we are always faced with ourselves. However, many qualities, such as intelligence or strength, are defined in relation to the performances of others. Moreover, accomplishments, such as setting records for the mile run or earning a B.A., often help to create a positive self-image, and accomplishments are measured against objective standards.

Strategies/Structures

1. Bradley's personal anecdote makes a point--that being famous means losing privacy--but, more importantly, the first person narrative establishes Bradley as a real person, not just a Knickerbocker uniform. A 5'11" drunk, even if he were an ex-boxer, would probably stand about as much chance against an NBA forward as the reporter on the airplane would have using his coat as a parachute. The other man respects Bradley's human right to privacy; the woman thinks Bradley is there for her convenience.

2. By linking all these contrasting elements in one sentence, Bradley implies that "fame" is not something one possesses but a condition under which

one lives. It intrudes into all aspects of one's life. The ellipses suggest that he is omitting any number of other examples of intrusions on his privacy.

3. Paragraphs 10 and 11 illustrate how athletes fit into Boorstin's category of "celebrities"; they are "for the moment" and are made by the media. By providing the illustration, Bradley integrates the quotation from Boorstin into his own essay by establishing the common rhetorical pattern of abstraction (Boorstin) and illustration or example (Bradley).

4. One might suppose that people who would buy an autobiography of a basketball star would tend to worship athletes. However, Bradley immediately challenges these readers: "There is no question...being a member of a successful...team is a mixed blessing." For his definition of a hero he quotes a scholarly historian, rather than a sportscaster. His own feelings about his celebrity status are ambivalent, if not wholly negative. He begins by using words with negative connotations, such as "notoriety," he refers to his "constant problem," and he concludes that most athletes realize only too late that "their sense of identity is insufficient."

Language

1. "Notoriety" (par. 6) means simply that people know who one is, but the word does have negative connotations (statesmen are famous; criminals are notorious). "Reacting instead of acting" means letting the circumstances dictate your actions instead of determining your own fate. In sports, it means you're letting the opponent set the pace; you're fighting his fight. "Forgetting how hot the subways are in August" means that a celebrity can afford to take taxis (a sign of status and wealth in New York), but he or she may be forgetting how most people have to live. "Having someone write you that if you visit this kid in the hospital he will get better" means that other people attribute miraculous powers to celebrities; it may also be an attempt to impose responsibility on the celebrity and to make him feel guilty if he doesn't

cooperate.

2. Bradley provides examples to show how fame has given him "access"--easy approach to people, services, and even sex.

JUDY SYFERS, "I Want a Wife"   (pp. 206-209)

Content

1. The purpose of a "wife" is to take care of all of the needs of her husband and children, without worrying too much about her own needs. She is a social secretary, a baby-sitter, a second income, a maid, and a mistress. Through it all, she is supposed to be understanding and non-complaining.

2. Syfers is trying to show that the division of labor between husbands and wives is often grossly unfair: the wives get all the dirty work. Syfers can expect to have feminists on her side, but some traditional women and some men might argue that she over-states her case. Some students will argue that marriages are no longer the way Syfers describes them.

3. No, Syfers does not favor the sexual double standard. Her apparent agreement with it is a form of hyperbole; her ironic tone serves to point out that her true views are opposite the ones she expresses here.

Strategies/Structures

1. The paragraphs describing the wife's duties recall a day in the life of a traditional wife: in the morning, she gets the children (and this husband) off to school; during the day, she runs errands and cleans house; in the afternoon, she listens to her husband's problems; in the evening, she entertains his friends; and, at night, she makes love to him--if he's not too tired. The irony of this organization is, of course, that we've been told that this wife is holding down a job. The point is that the typical day of a traditional wife is not

possible for a woman working outside the home as well.

2. The question is rhetorical; Syfers considers her point to be beyond argument and is implying one last time that "wife" is often treated as if it meant "personal servant." The expletive makes the rhetorical nature of the question even clearer.

3. Syfers wants to be sure that everyone understands a simple point: wives should not be treated as servants. Her appeal is to the emotions—and to a certain sense of humor—not particularly to the intellect. Ellison's appeal is more to the understanding, his problem more difficult to define, and his approach more philosophical. His language is necessarily more complex.

Language

1. Not using the personal pronoun suggests that the wife is not even a full person with personal wants and needs. Avoiding the feminine pronoun also impishly raises the possibility that a wife is not necessarily a woman; a "wife" is anyone who performs the duties described in the essay. This sets up the punch line at the end. Syfers could have a male "wife."

2. The short phrase "I want a wife" is both child-like and demanding. It implies that the person who keeps using it—the husband who wants a wife to take care of all his problems—is childish. Its frequent repetition shows that his demands may seem endless.

HANS C. VON BAEYER, "The Wonder of Gravity" (pp. 210-220)

Content

1. Both Newton and Einstein explain mathematically the way in which all objects in the universe attract one another. The greatest single difference between the two is that Newton assumes that space

is "absolute"; the attraction one body has for
   another can be measured against a "static"
   (unmoving) space which provides the stable
   reference point necessary for measurement.
   Einstein complicated the picture but made it more
   accurate by demonstrating that space is neither
   absolute nor static; space itself is in constant
   motion, so all measurement of motion must be
   relative.

2. Von Baeyer warns us in paragraph 2 that no mortal
   can ever answer the question, "What is gravity,"
   but we can say that "gravity" refers to the effect
   that every object in the universe exerts on every
   other object in the universe. Gravity determines
   how we are bound to the earth, the earth to the
   sun, the sun to the galaxy, the galaxy to the
   universe, and the universe unto itself. Thus, it
   is the organizing principle of the universe; it is
   the power which gives a shape and pattern to the
   spatial relationships that exist among all things.

3. Von Baeyer illustrates Einstein's concept of
   relative motion by asking us to imagine a stone
   floating--or at rest--in space. We can't tell if
   the stone is moving or is at rest unless we can
   measure its motion against an object--such as a
   star--which we assume to be at rest. Without this
   point of reference, we can't get our bearings and
   say whether or not motion is taking place. In a
   similar way, a train appears to move to a train
   conductor only because it is moving in relation to
   (in this case, towards) him. Once he has assumed
   himself to be a reference point, he can measure how
   quickly the motion of the train will bring it to
   him (par. 20).

Strategies/Structures

1. Von Baeyer is translating Einstein's language--the
   language of mathematics--into words and analogies,
   which comprise the language of his audience--people
   who are not scientists.

2. Von Baeyer avoids highly complicated scientific
   terminology because he is speaking to a general
   readership and not to scientists. Whether or not we
   really come to "understand" the concept of gravity,

we feel comfortable with his words and analogies because they are drawn from experiences that are common to all of us. Von Baeyer quotes Graves's poem for an obvious reason: he himself will use images (analogies) to help us think. There is also a subtle reason: the "he" in Graves's poem thinks in clear images. Newton's physics offers clearer images than does Einstein's physics. Relativity theory leads to images that are more like those of the "I" in Graves's poem. These images appear broken and less clear than those of Newtonian physics, even if they do offer more profound—and more accurate—insights.

3. Von Baeyer would not need to use analogies with other professional physicists, because they share the mathematical language of science. However, he might need to use some analogies with students because they probably would not have quite mastered the language of physics. With general readers, as we have seen, he uses only analogies. So, we see a continuum: the more specialized the audience, the more specialized the language; the more general the audience, the more general the language.

4. It's easy enough to imagine a stone floating in space—we've all seen such things in science fiction films. Whether or not the analogy actually explains anything is a more difficult question. As von Baeyer warns, no mortal can really understand "gravity." Some psychologists suggest that the word "understand" really refers to an emotional, not a cognitive process. At a certain point in a discussion, we "feel" as if we understand something, but the feeling may or may not have anything to do with a real intellectual grasp of the issue.

Language

1. Von Baeyer defines "natural" as "normal, healthy, ordinary" (par. 8). "Natural" is determined by contrast to that which is "pathological, in need of analysis." Notice that the words are taken from medicine. Doctors tend to analyze tissues only when they are afraid the tissue might be "unnatural." The problem with this, as von Baeyer points out, is that it "serves to end

conversations" which would explore and analyze how "normal," natural phenomena occur.

2. Von Baeyer doesn't use mathematics primarily because very few readers could follow Einstein's equations. Using them would not help to explain the subject. No "statement"--mathematical or verbal--no matter how "true" can help define a subject if the audience can't understand it.

LAIRD BLOOM, "The Progressives' Pilgrim"   (pp. 221-224)

Content

1. It seems obvious that a reviewer can't presuppose any prior knowledge of a book's content if his audience is unfamiliar with the work. However, this obvious point creates a difficult writing situation. The reviewer must provide an entire context in which the book can be understood, but he must do so very economically if he is to write a review and not another book. Bloom very quickly gives the essential facts about Wald (in par. 2-6). She was a nurse and later a reformer; she established a settlement and worked for labor reform. He wisely avoids biographical information that might be related but not essential: Wald's background, her philosophical convictions, her personal life, etc. His description of the Lower East Side is even more terse. He doesn't go into sociological, economic or political explanations. In a quick series of pictures (par. 2), he makes the essential point: here, people suffered.

2. No. More information would increase knowledge, but it is not necessary for understanding.

3. It is generally known that the lot of European immigrants to the United States was not an easy one, but an indication of the time in which Wald was working may suggest the types of problems she had to face.

4. Providing some anecdotes would perhaps give a better feeling for the book, but again, reviews are meant to be short. To repeat anecdotes would have occupied more space; the review's limited length

may dictate omission of some of the book's appealing features.

Strategies/Structures

1. A reviewer must make his opinion of a book clear, since people use reviews in determining whether or not a book is worth reading. Bloom's positive opinion of the author comes very quickly, in the first paragraph, but his opinion of the book isn't completely clear until paragraphs 7 and 8. This delay enforces an implicit point in the review: the book is more important as a record of Wald's accomplishment than as a piece of writing.

2. Horatio Alger novels and B-movies are easy to understand and sometimes enjoyable, but they are often not good works of art, primarily because of their sentimentality and implausible happy endings. One effect of this comparison is to suggest, diplomatically, that even if Bloom thinks highly of Wald's efforts at social reform, he's not going to heap praise upon her writing. If the reader doesn't understand the allusions, he should see the point when Bloom tells him that Wald's triumphs seem implausible, but the book works anyway.

3. Bloom gives a clear statement of the book's value in paragraphs 7 and 8: it is important as a record of what one person can do to help other people.

Language

1. Bloom does not formally define "progressive" or "progressivism," but perhaps he was wise not to do so. If he defined the terms in a formal, abstract way, he probably would not have avoided political terminology which would have distracted readers from his main point. Instead, in paragraphs 3 and 4, he wisely defined the terms from their practical results: lower mortality rates among children, laws regulating hours, pay, working conditions, etc.

2. In the first paragraph, Bloom refers to Wald as a

"practical friend." In the conclusion, he repeats the term "real": "real problems," "real people," "really possible," and finally "made the ideal a reality." These terms are very positive in an American society that prides itself on its realism and practicality. Conversely, as Bloom points out in paragraph 1, overly idealistic reformers are not often appreciated. Bloom, then, has taken the positive terms of practical America and used them to champion Wald.

DIVISION AND CLASSIFICATION

JAMES THURBER, "University Days" (pp. 231-238)

Content

1. Three specific references reveal the time period: in paragraph 3 the botany professor is compared to Lionel Barrymore; the modes of transportation suggested in paragraph 5 ("steam, horsedrawn, or electrically propelled") are somewhat dated; that World War I was being fought while he was a student gives the essay its firm time setting (par. 15). Mastering difficult subject matter, enduring impatient or indifferent professors, tolerating courses required for graduation, and knowing classmates who are "characters" are still a part of students' "University Days," and these subjects give this essay its timeless appeal. While students may point out how much more intelligent, ambitious, and goal-oriented they seem to be than those Thurber describes, they should be aware that the author has singled out exceptions for the sake of humor.

2. While he passed all courses but botany, Thurber candidly discusses his lackluster academic performance and his knack for irritating his professors. He was uninterested in economics (par. 5), physically inept in gym (par. 13), and "mediocre" in military drill (par. 16), and he cheated to pass swimming (par. 13). Bolenciecwcz was a miserable economics student, and Haskins had no flair for journalism, but they differed from Thurber (a botany failure) because they excelled in other areas. Bolenciecwcz was a star tackle (par. 5), and Haskins, an agriculture student, "knew animals" (par. 14), but Thurber tells only of his mistakes, disappointments, and failures. These characters are funny because Thurber shows them in two isolated situations that allow Thurber (and the reader) to feel temporary superiority in the midst of another's folly.

3. The botany professor loses patience with Thurber while Bassum spoonfeeds answers to the football hero. The insensitive gym instructor makes students strip and "snaps" questions at them, and senile, short-tempered Littlefield should have been at Gettysburg rather than Ohio State. These are stereotypes. The botanist, a "man of science," is singleminded; the indifferent swimming teacher doesn't know his students; the General is more concerned with order than substance in his troops. Thurber exaggerates his professors' characteristics to show humorously how he was victimized by these seeming lunatics (in paragraph 4 the botany professor "screamed, losing control"; in paragraph 5 Bassum must prompt Bolenciecwcz with sound effects; in paragraph 18 General Littlefield does combat with flies and forgets why he summoned Thurber). By stressing their collective oddities, Thurber evokes sympathy for himself.

Strategies/Structures

1. See Division and Classification introduction in text.

2. Thurber, the student, was too close to these painful, embarrassing situations to see them objectively; he didn't know then that he would survive his failures. Thurber, the writer, knew he had survived; time and success had mellowed his recollections. The audience, also survivors of their own mishaps, laughs with him now as he makes fun of his former self.

3. Each example illustrates Thurber's or a classmate's anguish and frustration in the college setting (the botany story that spans his two years of failure, Bassum's question that seems to stump the football star, Haskins's long-awaited scoop on the horses' sores, Littlefield's commendation that never comes once Thurber interrupts his war games with the flies). Each vignette presents a comic resolution to the vignette's tense situation.

4. A possible implicit thesis of Thurber's essay might be, "In my student days at Ohio State, the professors were nearly as incompetent as the students." This message is implied in the examples

he uses since each is humiliating to him or someone
else. Since classification essays are composed of
categories illustrated with convincing examples,
the strength of the examples should lead the reader
to the author's conclusion without more needing to
be said. An explicit thesis would merely state the
obvious.

Language

1. "The familiar lateral opacity" is so formal that
    it's out of place, and is therefore humorous. It
    enhances the other humor.

2. Thurber uses other complicated language;
    "variegated constellation" (par. 4) is, again, out
    of place and adds to the humor. Bassum, the
    economics professor, is a timid man whose formal
    language ("'any medium, agency, or method of going
    from one place to another,'" par. 5) exaggerates
    his formal teaching style. This provides a
    dramatically humorous contrast to his embarrassed
    hint of "Choo-choo-choo"--in highly informal
    language--to help Bolenciecwcz answer the
    elementary question.

LINDA FLOWER, "Writing for an Audience"   (pp. 238-243)

Content

1. If the writer has a specific reader or group of
    readers in mind, he or she probably knows the
    answer to the questions Flower asks in paragraph 2.
    If the intended audience is more general or unknown
    to the writer, he'll have to estimate the amount of
    knowledge the reader already has about the subject
    and supply sufficient background information to
    fill in the gaps.

2. Not only is it possible for a writer to understand
    another's views, it is also necessary and only
    fair. If the writer expects the reader to see
    different sides of an issue, the writer has to
    acknowledge that there are different sides. While
    certainty of fairness can't always be guaranteed,

the writer should ask, "Can I at least understand if not agree with viewpoints on this issue that differ from my own?"

3. Awareness of the reader's age, sex, race, economic situation, political interests, education, as well as knowledge of and attitude toward a particular subject may help the writer determine and adapt to an audience's needs. Student writers won't know their readers' needs until they know who their readers are (a professor, an employer, the student body, parents, a friend).

4. Flower's chart presents a situation in which a new bookstore manager is to become the primary audience for a student employee (the writer). Perhaps the employee has been asked to write out a job description for the new boss. Each category helps the employee know more about the employer before doing any writing. In column I (KNOWLEDGE), the employee notes the new manager has limited knowledge of the bookstore's operation and has no knowledge of the employee's added responsibilities. Column II (ATTITUDE) shows the manager's negative attitude ("image") surrounding the employee's job: it has little responsibility, and it is only temporary. The information in these two columns would tell the employee of the gaps that need to bridged before the employer can see things the employee's way. Column III (NEEDS) indicates what the employee must include to establish "common ground." By telling the manager not only the tasks but the time and expertise required for each, the employee may change the manager's attitude about the job.

Strategies/Structures

1. Flower knows they have some knowledge, but to make them understand composition better, she has classified the three areas that separate the writer from the audience and has illustrated each with examples students can identify with. She briefly reiterates what she thinks her readers already know but defines and illustrates attitudes and needs.

2. Writing is a means of sharing information with others and is a valuable activity. It is also a

powerful activity in which the writer can "create a
momentary common ground" (par. 1) and cause
another to see things as he sees them. Because she
is writing to students who don't yet know how to
create that common ground, her assumption is that
students have an uncertain attitude toward writing
and need to know workable strategies for solving the
problems that writing presents (par. 10).

3. Flower spends the least amount of space on
knowledge and the most on needs because knowledge
is the easiest to ascertain and "to handle" (par.
3); needs are less obvious, more varied; they
require more adaptation from the writer and
consequently, more explanation from Flower, who is
addressing the writer. She arranges the parts in
order of increasing length and complexity of
explanation.

Language

1. Flower defines these terms implicity, rather than
explicitly. She sees knowledge as facts coupled
with attitudes; the two aren't mutually exclusive.
Her knowledge of lakes, for instance, is composed
of neutral associations ("fishing, water skiing,
stalled outboards") darkened by others that are
unpleasant ("cloudy skies, long rainy days, and
feeling generally cold and damp"). Our factual
knowledge of a subject is colored by the image
("loose cluster of associations") we have of it.
"Needs," Flower implies in paragraphs 7-10, refers
to specific unsolved problems; a need can be met by
a specific application of knowledge that solves the
problem.

2. "Primary audience" here means the most likely
intended reader of one's writing. In a
non-academic setting this might be the reader whose
problem needs to be solved through the knowledge
the writer imparts, but in an academic setting the
primary audience is likely to be the teacher who
assigns the paper. A secondary audience would have
less immediate need to obtain such knowledge, but
might be interested in the theory or implications
of the knowledge imparted.

3. Several references to college indicate that Flower

is writing primarily to college composition
students (par. 7--a friend majoring in biology; par.
9--a college writing assignment, par. 10--reference
to bluebooks). Based on her vocabulary,
definitions, and examples, Flower is addressing
those who already know the fundamentals of writing
but need to learn strategies for approaching their
subject and their audience. Flower's secondary
audience is teachers who assign the textbook from
which this selection is taken.

LEWIS THOMAS, "The Technology of Medicine"   (pp. 243-250)

Content

1. Thomas views the present treatment of illness by
   medical professionals as an industrial, mechanical
   practice rather than a science that studies the
   causes of illness. Too often the physician is a
   repairman rather than a scientist who prevents
   illness from occurring. Thomas saves the word
   "science" for the final sentence in order to remind
   readers of the importance of his message: medicine
   is a science and should be treated as such.

1. Supportive therapy is auxiliary treatment given to
   patients who have illnesses that "are not, by and
   large, understood." It would include such measures
   as psychological counseling, pastoral care, at-home
   nursing, or any of the other services designed to
   help patients cope with illness. Thomas doesn't
   consider such measures technological because they
   aren't aimed at the discovery or elimination of
   what caused the illness in the first place.

2. Like nontechnology, the aim of halfway technology
   is not to discover or eliminate causes of disease
   but is to help patients live with the
   "incapacitating effects of certain diseases." It
   is primitive because it overlooks the major problem
   of understanding how the disease has originated.

3. Thomas favors the third type because it is the only
   one to actively address the problem of what causes
   disease. While the other two levels involve *ex
   post facto* treatment, level three seeks to

eradicate the need for anything other than prevention. The public takes for granted this level because it has so effectively removed these threats to our health.

4. Basic research refers to the study of what causes illness. Once the causes are known, in most cases there would be no need for the other levels of technology, and the cost of health care would decrease. Thomas cites particular examples of previously fatal diseases, such as pulmonary tuberculosis, now controlled through preventive medicine. He has indicated that the bulk of medical costs is generated by the first two levels of technology, and he leads the reader to see how inexpensive prevention could be in comparison.

Strategies/Structures

1. See Division and Classification introduction in text, p. 229.

2. Thomas moves from the least to the most effective technology to emphasize the need for more research. Since the main message is that preventive medicine saves lives and money, he leads the reader to this point in the final paragraph. Any alteration would have weakened his argument by putting the emphasis on auxiliary treatment, not preventive medicine.

3. Thomas's thesis is found in paragraph 17, near the end of the essay. He waits until this point so that, after having presented his case against the inadequacies of the first two levels, he can leave the reader with the message that he most wants to be retained.

Language

1. The "science of medicine," Thomas implies in the last paragraph (par. 20), is that which leads to a "genuine understanding of the causes and manifestations of disease," or of "disease mechanisms" (par. 17). Technology, whether "the real high technology of medicine" (par. 17) or "halfway technology" (par. 10), refers to the

management of disease mechanisms.

2. For the most part, Thomas discusses diseases and health problems with which general readers would be familiar (cancer, pneumonia, typhoid, arthritis) in non-tecnhical language. When his language gets more technical he may momentarily exceed such readers' understanding, but he usually provides a translation into lay language by the end of a given paragraph. Thus, in paragraph 12 the "chronic glomerulonephritis" of sentence 2 is identified as a kidney problem in sentence 3.

ROBERT BRUSTEIN, "Reflections on Horror Movies" (pp. 250-261)

Content

1. The three categories reveal the changing roles of the scientist and monster. The Mad Doctor genre shows the scientist creating havoc in an attempt to play God. The Atomic Beast films show the humanitarian scientist undoing the damage caused by other, less scrupulous scientists. The scientist in the third group is both evildoer and savior. The classification system enables Brustein to explain how filmmakers present scientific research as something evil or good or both.

2. Without the monster there would be no conflict whereby the scientist could prove himself a man of conscience or an egomaniac. The Mad Doctor label clearly identifies the scientist's villainy since he moves the monster to evil actions. The Atomic Beast carries two implications: the monster is a beast from the outset, but it is a beast because it's atomic--a condition imposed on it at some point by an irresponsible scientist. While not inherently evil, the scientist--and consequently, humankind, which the scientist represents--must pay for his curiosity.

3. The moral question is whether scientific research is good or bad. How far can scientists go before they start tampering with those things best left alone? Brustein feels this too weighty an issue to be justly presented in films since the subject

"needs more articulate treatment than the covert and superstitious way it is handled in horror movies" (par. 18). Films intended primarily for entertainment can't be expected to deal extensively with such issues because they "engage the spectator's feelings without making any serious demand on his mind" (par. 1).

4. As shown in horror films, power stemming from knowledge is disastrous because the powerful can't differentiate between good and evil. While Americans tend to revere certain types of power, whether in the athletic arena or on the battlefield, the intellectual power represented in such movies is frightening because the fate of many is placed undemocratically in the hands of one self-serving individual who is often more concerned with satisfying his own intellectual curiosity than helping his fellow man.

Strategies/Structures

1. A horror film fan would not need Brustein's plot summaries. Brustein is writing for those who either can't understand their popularity or haven't seen enough of them to recognize their similarities and differences. The reader doesn't need to know much about the subject, since Brustein includes representative plots from each class that support his statements.

2. Within the Mad Doctor class he describes teenage monster films that show a scientist manipulating a victim with whom a predominantly adolescent audience could identify. Under Atomic Beast he discusses particular films that again show individuals actively victimized by science; in some, the beast's size is altered; in others, the scientist becomes shrunken or enlarged. The sub-groups fortify the major classes and allow for more specific films to be included in the discussion.

3. The discussion begins with the Mad Doctor class because it has been in existence the longest. Since these films evolved from European folk tales, the reader can understand the transfer of superstition from moors to laboratory. The changing role of the scientist reflects the

audience's change in attitude about science. When audiences were skeptical about scientific research, they were treated to Mad Doctor films that confirmed their worst suspicions. When scientific advancements made audiences more favorably disposed to what was being done in research labs, the Atomic Beast films provided a scientist who was the hero/savior. Recent developments (test-tube babies, organ transplants, Nobel Prize winners' sperm banks) have brought into question how far science can go within the bounds of morality; thus, Interplanetary Monster films show "the public's ambivalence towards science" (par. 16). (See also the answer to Content, question 1.) The presentation of Brustein's classes shows that despite their shoddy quality, horror movies are popular with American audiences because they tap into fears people have about scientific experimentation.

Language

1. Brustein's labels ("Mad Doctor," "Atomic Beast," "Interplanetary Monster") are appropriate and descriptive labels for the categories he establishes, and they are suitably restrictive so that the categories do not overlap for purposes of discussion.

ILLUSTRATION AND EXAMPLE

JOAN DIDION, "Marrying Absurd" (pp. 268-272)

Content

1. In paragraph 1, Didion informs the reader that one can get a marriage license in the middle of the night. In paragraph 3 she tells us that services are "offered twenty-four hours a day, seven days a week." In paragraph 4 she talks about weddings being held all day and all night, and she concludes with the detail of a chapel sign that says, "one moment, please."

2. Didion realistically describes approaching Las Vegas from L.A. Las Vegas does appear "like a mirage on the horizon" (par. 1); it is literally in the middle of a desert, which is an unlikely place to build a town. As Didion points out, there is no historical, economic, or geographic reason for the location of Las Vegas.

3. No. If she did, the weddings would not strike her as absurd. Her example of the show-girl who had to rush from the ceremony to get the sitter and then make it to the midnight show supports the idea that some patrons do believe in the craps analogy.

4. The pregnant, underage bride—and her joy at the "niceness" of her wedding—indeed represent a "facsimile of proper ritual." It is unlikely that the reader considers this to be the "proper" way to conduct a marriage, and the bride's emotional comment that it was as nice as she had dreamed it would be is an ironic one. She has bought the "niceness" that Las Vegas is selling without recognizing that she has done so.

Strategies/Structures

1. As Camus explained, nothing is absurd in itself. "The absurd" resides in the conflict between our

expectations of something and the reality. If the judge thought of people as cattle, there would be nothing absurd about marrying sixty-seven couples in three minutes. What is absurd is his notion that a three-minute ceremony is more meaningful than marrying en masse. Didion needs to establish this quickly, since Las Vegas weddings are absurd only when the people who go through them are expecting something meaningful.

2. If one associates "Getting Married" with romantic landscapes, the rattlesnakes and mesquite are one more absurdity; there is no relationship, literal or symbolic, between the environment and the activity. Indeed, they are antithetical, as Didion's labeling of the desert as "hostile" (par. 2) indicates. The wedding party in full finery having formal photographs taken in a motel parking lot is another such incongruity.

3. The stepfather (rather than the natural father) who is giving away the bride indicates how far removed from the traditional family our society has become.

4. The drunkenness of the bride shows how out of control these people are, and the coarseness of her groom shows the lack of sensitivity in their lives. The couple illustrates the lack of commitment to a marriage that is in its nature impulsive and presumably transitory.

5. Didion obviously thinks these weddings are absurd, but her tone is certainly that of a person bemused--even amused--certainly not outraged by the behavior. Didion could be accused of being snobbish and condescending, but there is also a note of genuine sadness in her ultimate comment: "it is...facsimile of proper ritual, to children who do not know how else to find it, how to make the arrangements, how to do it 'right'" (par. 4). Her intended audience is expected to agree with her view, and consequently is probably composed of people who would not get married in Las Vegas.

Language

1. Didion is imitating the language of a fashion

show—appropriately, since this wedding seems more like a show than a meaningful ceremony. By not separating the modifiers with commas, Didion is further imitating the way a fashion show emcee's voice runs on; no word is more important than any other.

2. Didion allows Las Vegas to damn itself with its own words. The inanity of the advertising reveals its own absurdity as well as Didion could in her own words. The commercial aspects of advertising wedding servides and paraphernalia undercut the solemnity and sentimentality traditionally associated with weddings in more conventional settings.

LOREN EISELEY, "The Brown Wasps"   (pp. 272-281)

Content

1. Eiseley's thesis is that all living creatures create in their minds an image of home—a place of security and shelter. All of the men and animals that Eiseley describes have such an image in their minds, and all of them cling to the image after the reality is gone; they seem to prove his thesis.

2. By seeing that animals and insects behave in ways surprisingly similar to ours, we learn that many of our behavior patterns are perfectly "natural." It is perfectly natural for people—as well as other animals—to search for a home, so we should be more understanding of bums who hang around train stations (and wasps that nest in our attics!). The blind man had been nourished and supported by those who rode the El, just as had the pigeons. The El had been a "food-bearing river" for both.

3. The real world for Eiseley seems to be the image of "home" that we carry within our minds or subconscious imagination. It continues, real and permanent, even after the external reality has changed.

4. The mouse in Eiseley's apartment might not be the identical mouse Eiseley saw in the nearby field; Eiseley admits it might have been "one of his

fellows." It doesn't matter, since the mouse is being used only as an example. Ultimately, whether or not Eiseley is justified in interpreting the mouse in human terms is debatable, but the force of his essay is to convince us that he is justified: "homing" is natural to man and all other creatures as well.

5. Eiseley admits that our mental pictures of home are sometimes inaccurate—we are "out of touch." Even so, the images remain in our minds permanently even after the world changes, the Els and fields are gone, and the trees are dead.

Strategies/Structures

1. Eiseley describes the old men from the point of view of a detached observer, and they are presented in relation to a policeman, a representative in our society of the "objective" observer. When he describes the mouse, he uses the point of view of an involved participant and tries to enter into the mous 's mind. He is again at least emotionally invol ed when he observes the pigeons, and by the end of the essay, Eiseley the author is looking directly at himself as a child.

2. Eiseley isolates the one sentence to show us how dramatic the impact is when one's home is suddenly wiped away. The sentence would not carry the impact if it were integrated into the paragraph.

3. Although the order of the illustrations at first seems random, there is a clear drift from detached observation to emotional involvement (see answer to question 1). The concluding example has the most poignant personal associations, for the author at any rate.

Language

1. Wasps are essentially nesting creatures, and we quickly associate them with their nests, their "homes." This association is very appropriate for Eiseley's essay. We don't as quickly associate field mice with their holes, and, even though we

might think of pigeons having a strong sense of home ("homing pigeons"), we don't associate them with the communal homes that wasps share.

2. The language is obviously human. Even if mice used words, only the more poetic ones would think of "the shuttered daylight for an hour." Eiseley's point still stands, however; all species have their own images of home, whether or not they can express them in words.

MINORU YAMASAKI, "The Aesthetics and Practice of Architecture" (pp. 281-289)

Content

1. Yamasaki's illustrations show the variety of ways architecture can achieve its purpose. He mentions the paper and wood houses of Japan and the stone buildings of Europe (par. 8), the cathedrals of Europe (par. 7) and the wandering Japanese temples (par. 10), the delights of Japanese gardens (par. 3) and his own World Trade Center (par. 11).

2. In paragraph 2, Yamasaki discusses "the softness of wood and plaster" which impart more of a "human feeling" than "brick, concrete, or stone." In paragraph 11, he makes some perceptive comments about how "all glass" buildings can make people feel very uncomfortable.

3. From Yamasaki's views, one might expect his buildings to be simple, almost delicate, "surprising," interesting, and comfortable to be in. Perhaps the World Trade Center is a better example of the problems Yamasaki discusses than the goals he has set for himself. The lines of the two towers are classic and simple, but they are huge and imposing at the same time. They don't surprise us with their variety--they look like most skyscrapers--and such details as the three-story elevator lobby may make visitors feel dwarfed and uncomfortable.

4. Obviously (par. 1) Yamasaki has been very much influenced by Japanese architecture: he sees its standards as those modern architects should strive

for. Since Yamasaki talks about being in Japan and is clearly very knowledgeable about Japan, his name probably indicates that he is Japanese. Nevertheless, it should also be pointed out that the same essay could have been written by an American (or a person of any other nationality) who had studied and lived in Japan and had absorbed that country's culture, which is, indeed, Yamasaki's own life story.

Strategies/Structures

1. If Yamasaki had been writing for architects, he would not have had to define an "all glass" building or "weathering steel," and he probably would not have given the historical background that he provides in paragraphs 5 and 10. The fact that he did provide these explanations and background allows people without a knowledge of architecture to understand the essay.

2. A deer, a race horse, an athlete, or a dancer appears graceful and beautiful because we can see the natural porportions and lines of the body. If these natural lines are covered up by layers of fat--as in the case of a pig, a hippopotamus, or an obese person--this natural grace may be obscured. The same is true in architecture; the lines should be clean, pure, and uncluttered. The choices of animals are appropriate, since most people find deer lovely but consider the hippopotamus to be somewhat ungainly.

3. Yamasaki's aesthetic taste seems to run toward the understated, the civilized, and the humane. Passionate rantings and ravings would have been at cross purposes to his thesis and would have made his essay less convincing.

Language

1. Yamasaki didn't explicitly define these terms because he was speaking about general aesthetic principles. If he had been speaking about a specific building, he could have told us what specific "delicate elements" might be included in

it, but, since the specific meanings of each of these terms would differ in each building, Yamasaki is forced to leave these terms in a general form. Presumably, each reader has his own general sense of what these terms mean.

CARL SAGAN, "The Cosmic Calendar" (pp. 289-295)

Content

1. Sagan allows one calendar year to stand for all time since the "beginning" of the universe (at least, the universe as we know it). Having done that, he can assign cosmic events to certain dates, giving us an idea of the relative time between events. The year is the most appropriate basis for comparison for two reasons. First, a year is a small enough segment of time for us to imagine easily; few of us can easily think in decades, since ten years seems so long to us, and very few of us live a century. The second reason for using a year is that it is our basic measure of time: decades and centuries are collections of years.

2. Besides the analogies of the year, months, and even seconds, Sagan uses the analogy of "weaving a tapestry" of the history of life (par. 3). That analogy might seem merely a figure of speech, but it carries an important message: this kind of "history" is, in some ways, speculative, conjectured, and interpretive; it is art almost as much as it is science.

3. The diagrams tell us the specifics, which events took place during particular months and days, even seconds (on December 31); for the most part, the prose section only explains the analogy and gives very few illustrations. The diagrams--particularly the calendar for December--allow us to form a visual image which reinforces the conceptual explanations of the prose. Once we've understood the analogy, the diagrams are very useful as illustrations, but, of course, if we had not read the explanation of the analogy, little of Sagan's illustration would make much sense.

Strategies/Structures

1. Moving from the remote past to the present is the clearest way for Sagan to proceed. Since we all know something about the present, we know where the chronology is heading, and we can follow it as easily as we can follow a murder mystery when we have already been told the ending. This order also serves another purpose. By beginning with what we don't know and moving to what we do know, Sagan creates a feeling of optimism-- we are "figuring things out." If he moved in the opposite direction, he would have been forced to conclude with the murky unknowns of the beginnings of the universe.

2. The obvious limitation of the analogy is that the universe wasn't completed in a year. In compressing these cosmic events into a framework we can understand, Sagan runs the risk that we will develop a distorted notion of how quickly these events occur. The analogy also imposes precision and order on a process extending over a vast time period in which dates of events are approximated (and may involve centuries or millenia) and are not determined as easily as the analogy's compression implies.

Language

1. We really don't need to understand "geological stratification" or "radioactive dating" as long as we understand that Sagan is saying that we do have scientific ways of dating cosmic events. All we need to know about the Big Bang is what Sagan tells us; it is the prevailing scientific theory of the beginning of the universe, and it happened a very long time ago.

2. The first sentence in its childlike simplicity reinforces its own content: human beings are very young. As a species, we are infants of the universe. The fairy-tale-like simplicity is also appropriate to the contents that follow: this is a myth to help us understand something about "the beginning." The sentence also calms us before we are confronted by the potentially intimidating

material. Finally, the sentence is appropriately humble. As Sagan later says, "The construction of such tables and calendars is inevitably humbling" (par. 5).

LAI MAN LEE, "My Bracelet"   (pp. 295-298)

Content

1. In general, these bracelets symbolize good luck.

2. Lee's bracelet has come to symbolize, for her, her relationship with her parents, their love for her, her Chinese heritage, its traditions, and, of course, good luck. Having that much sense of family, love, and tradition is lucky.

3. The timing was perfect, for it taught Lee that their love for her is absolute; it is not a reward for her being "good."

Strategies/Structures

1. By beginning with the the bracelet itself, Lee gives the readers a visual image that they can keep in mind throughout the essay. The image can then pick up new associations, just as the real object can.

2. Lee begins with description (par. 1), proceeds mostly by chronology (par. 2-5), and concludes with an evaluation.

3. If Lee's audience were Chinese, she would not need to explain Chinese customs (just as Yamasaki would not have needed to explain architectural terms if he had been writing for architects; see question 1, Strategies/Structures of the Yamasaki section, this chapter).

4. Some of the paragraphs do seem short; paragraphs 2 and 3 could be combined, as could paragraphs 4 and 5, since each pair of paragraphs deals with related events. However, as it stands, each paragraph break represents a passage of time, and the author

might want to preserve that.

Language

1. Yes, because the emotions expressed are powerful but very simple and straightforward. Powerful symbols are often very simple: a wedding ring, the cross, the star of David, the moon, and the lotus.

2. "Sentiment" is derived from the Latin word "to feel" and the noun for the mind. A person of sentiment, then, is one whose mind not only thinks but feels. Lee obviously feels, so her essay shows sentiment. "Sentimental," however, is a term used to refer to feelings that seem excessive in relation to the subject at hand. It is an act of sentiment to cry at the death of one's parent; it is sentimental to cry at the death of a neighbor's goldfish. But is it sentimental to cry at the death of one's pet dog? The question of appropriateness is a difficult one. Lee's essay is only sentimental if one judges that she has too much feeling for her subjects. For instance, the reader may find her treatment of her bracelet to be sentimental, while her feelings for her parents may seem more appropriate sentiments.

COMPARISON AND CONTRAST

BARRY LOPEZ, "My Horse" (pp. 305-313)

Content

1. The main subject is his truck, but he gives the essay this title because of the similarities his Dodge van shares with his horse Coke High, as well as with other horses. To him the truck is a horse of sorts because of its animation, willfulness, and heart.

2. Both truck and horse are modes of transportation that can be used for one's occupation or recreation. Both are valuable possessions to their owners, and both have distinguishing features (size, shape, color, speed, "heart"). Explicit comparisons are made between the Indians' custom of tying turquoise onto their horses and his keeping the piece of turquoise in the van (par. 8), the dents of the van (par. 12), and those similar marks on his horse (par. 13), the difference in the distance each can be taken (par. 13), the amount of cargo he transports in each (par. 14), the improvements he's thought to make on each (par. 17), his communication with each (par. 18-21), and the accidents he's had with each (par. 26-28). He implies a comparison between the name of his truck and the names poeple give horses (par. 10-11) and the aloofness of each (par. 30). Besides a horse, he also compares his van to a competitor (par. 33), to the wolves it is transporting on one occasion (par. 29), and to rolling water (par. 22).

3. The reader needs little knowledge to understand the comparison. From the essay we learn of the author's many likes (his van, horses, wolves, travel, nature, simplicity) and dislikes (concern with materialism, things that aren't utilitarian, people who don't reciprocate his kindness), and he honestly reveals an aspect of his nature that doesn't please him (par. 27--kicking the van's door).

4. The wolves are mentioned twice to stress their importance to him. The anecdote reveals his love of animals and at the same time shows his solitary and even mysterious nature. The van's responsiveness to its cargo is an illustration of its "heart" and further serves his comparison of animal and machine. The purpose of the mission goes unexplained since it is unnecessary to his purpose of presenting a comparison, and the incident itself generates interest by its very mysteriousness.

Strategies/Structures

1. Lopez begins by explaining the value of the Indians' horses to establish their importance. This in turn is the basis for his discussion of the van's importance. The reader has little difficulty seeing the connection between these items. Paragraphs 7 and 35 are similar in their reference to the raised arm of the warrior and the Indian war cry "Hoka hey!" He suggests in paragraph 35 that his response when the van ceases to function will parallel that of the warrior who either fights or moves on when confronted with the inevitable.

2. The departures from standard compositional forms enable Lopez to be conversational and personal in his essay. The message becomes reminiscent of the cowboy's yarn told around a campfire on an open plain.

3. Each narrative serves as an example in his comparison, and they are presented in the form of anecdotes. Many of the anecdotes have a clear structure of a line of action proceeding within a single paragraph from the beginning to the middle to a climax near the paragraph's end (see par. 26, 27, 28, 29).

4. A horse can't carry the amount of cargo a van can (par. 15), but the van doesn't respond to affection the way Coke did (par. 19). By including differences, Lopez becomes a believable writer: nothing is one-sided or perfect. He mentions the faults of each to make the reader believe even more in his truthfulness.

5. Lopez uses Detroit in paragraph 32 to symbolize the builders of automotive machinery without "heart" and without an understanding of "heart."

Language

1. People name an object to make it more personal and to establish the object's personality and individuality. Like the Indians, Lopez would prefer anonymity for his "horse." Since the van is an extension of himself, it needs no other name. Because the name came with the van and is generic, Lopez finds "Dodge" an unobtrusive label, as insignificant as any other.

2. Examples of similes include "Transporting timber wolves by truck was like moving clouds across the desert" (par. 16) and "You roll like water when you drive by moonlight on a hilly Kentucky road" (par. 22). These paint a vivid picture of the actions he wants to describe.

BRUCE CATTON, "Grant and Lee" (pp. 313-319)

Content

1. As one of the landed gentry, Lee was a reflection of his Southern heritage and culture. He represented the old order that admired and revered past traditions, idealism, education, wealth, grace, and a chivalric sense of duty (noblesse oblige) that precluded a classless social structure. Its endurance made the thought of change insupportable. Grant represented the new culture of the West that encouraged and demanded self-reliance, grit, opportunism, change, and growth. Unlike Lee, Grant reflected a part of America that recognized growth wasn't possible without change.

2. While Lee was strengthened by his sense of obligation to the land and those who worked it, his adherence to past traditions overrode concern for the future growth of America. In contrast, Grant's determination to see the democratic promise of

equality fulfilled overlooked the fact that long-established traditions don't die out quickly.

3. Both were excellent fighters (par. 3), had "tenacity and fidelity" (par. 14) regarding their respective causes, possessed speed and intelligence (par. 15), and could recognize when a fight was over (par. 16). Because they were both hard but fair fighters, their sportsmanlike and statesmanlike behavior enhanced the chance for re-establishment of peace.

4. People's very survival has always depended on their ability to adapt or change when necessary. Because the South was grounded in a mentality that resisted change, Catton suggests it was doomed to failure. Conversely, the side favoring change for the sake of growth was destined to survive.

Strategies/Structures

1. The strategy of the essay is to proceed from the differences between the two men to their similarities as a way of showing how reconciliation could be effected at the end of the Civil War. If the essay had begun by establishing the basis for reconciliation, there would have been no climax or resolution to lead up to.

2. Only four of the 16 paragraphs are dedicated to Lee and Grant's shared similarities, while the bulk of the essay concentrates on their differences. This imbalance reflects the differences that led to the Civil War, as symbolized by the dissimilarities between Lee and Grant both as individuals and as representatives of two distinct cultures.

3. Catton's references to their respective backgrounds and beliefs establish Lee and Grant as symbols of their cultures. He provides very little about them as individuals (nothing about appearance, habits, speech, age, behavior), but such information would have been irrelevant considering Catton's purpose.

4. The references to the surrender convey Catton's message of hope about this contrast in mentalities. While the contrast ultimately widened into conflict, the author begins and ends with a

reminder that the outcome was peaceful and ushered in "a great new chapter" in American history.

Language

1. The Lee family's origins could be traced back to the settling of Virginia. Tidewater refers to the coastal section of the state (Jamestown/Williamsburg/Yorktown) first colonized by English settlers. The reference serves to establish the Lee's longevity as residents of this area. Because these colonists were English, the references to chivalric behavior serve to fortify the image of Lee descending from aristocratic British forebears. The image is ambiguous, since chivalry was a noble concept, though impractical and anachronistic in a newly-democratic nation.

2. All are lofty, emotion-packed words that reflect the idealism and dedication of both sides in this conflict.

SUZANNE BRITT JORDAN, "That Lean and Hungry Look"   (pp. 319-323)

Content

1. Jordan does stereotype these two groups, largely for the sake of humor. The stereotypes, however, enable her readers to identify with at least some of the qualities she mentions regarding both groups. In paragraph 9 she individualizes her subject somewhat when she discusses the thin person at the jigsaw puzzle party.

2. Jordan has obviously left other characteristics out since they might have detracted from her humorous purpose. By excluding such topics as health, she keeps her tone light and keeps her audience focused on the humor. Thin people aren't treated fairly, but she doesn't want to present them fairly since she is in sympathy with the fat people. A current popular slogan states, "You can never be too rich or too thin." Since thin people rarely experience the ridicule or ostracism suffered by the

overweight, Jordan's aim is to praise the attributes of fat while taking a swipe at the thin.

3. This is a matter of personal opinion.

4. Perhaps both groups are concerned about what others think about them, want to look attractive, and may have difficulty finding clothes that fit well. Finally, both groups are sometimes limited in their activities (participation in certain sports, for example). All of these concerns that might be mutually shared are sometimes related to one's weight.

5. If Jordan had added one more type she would have destroyed the effectiveness and force of her contrast. She clearly wants to show the virtues of being heavy, and she does this by holding up this group against its extreme opposite.

Strategies/Structures

1. Jordan supports her generalizations with humorous examples. Thin people are crunchy, like the carrots they eat (par. 4). Fat people know life is illogical and unjust, for if God were just He'd give them donuts (par. 6). These examples are adapted to the nature and personality of the types Jordan is describing.

2. From the outset the humor is obvious. Jordan's five subcategories of thin people in paragraph 1 immediately establish her humorous tone. Since she is pointing out the good-natured, happy, lovable qualities of the overweight, her humor reinforces this point.

3. The puzzle group example establishes her credibility since she's had first-hand experience in viewing representatives from both groups at the same time. Her illustration is intended to let the reader know she's speaking with some authority, and that her values favor fun and group participation over logic and efficiency.

Language

1. Alliteration is a form of word play, and her use of it reflects the disposition of the fat. The thin don't enjoy word play; they like phrases (par. 2--"not enough hours in a day; par. 3--"tackle" a task; par. 4--"the key thing"). Jordan cleverly uses words that begin with the fat letter "g," and the words themselves help create the impression of jolly, jello-y, unstable happiness and goodness she associates with the heavyweights.

2. Jordan's language choice is playful, unserious, understandable, down-to-earth, and fun; all are qualities she associates with fat people.

JAMES AGEE, "Comedy's Greatest Era" (pp. 323-333)

Content

1. How these comedians used and dressed their bodies sparked laughter. The baggy-suited Tramp twitched his mustache and showed "what a human is, and is up against" (par. 3). A master of mime, Chaplin revealed through movement, glance, and gesture his attitudes towards gags leveled against him. Lloyd's humor relied on a situation, embarrassing or terrifying to whichever horn-rimmed character he played, and topping the gag was his forte. Keaton's was pure physical comedy stripped of emotion and sentiment. His unchanging deadpan expression was as funny in its constancy as was Chaplin's exaggerated emotionalism.

2. Agee points out that by not smiling, Keaton drew immediate attention to himself, the victim of all the jokes. The deadpan was a device used to play the "laughs against it" (par. 17).

3. Their choice of what to do with their bodies varied. Each used a different facial feature to humorous advantage (Chaplin's mustache, Lloyd's teeth, Keaton's vacant gaze). Their costume choice also differed (Chaplin's shoddy hat and suit, Lloyd's too-small clothes and owlish glasses, Keaton's flat hat). But their most noticeable

difference was their reaction to a gag. Chaplin's response was emotional, sometimes poignant. Lloyd became its master rather than victim. Keaton passively surrendered to it.

4. Their humor in the absence of sound reveals their skill as physical comedians. Each produced laughter by his very presence, without the aid of a single word. This talent isn't fully appreciated by audiences nurtured on verbal humor, which talkies made possible. Through his explanation of their accomplishments within the limitations of silent films, Agee makes a strong case supporting their genius. He might find merit in the efforts of Allen, Sellers, Belushi, and Brooks since much of their humor relies on visual gags made popular by these silent pioneers.

5. While the silent film buff would have an advantage in recalling these moments, Agee's precise, evocative descriptions are enough, even for those unfamiliar with this genre.

Strategies/Structures

1. Almost every paragraph contains narrations that double as illustrations. Chaplin's poetry is revealed in *One A.M.* as he drunkenly heads to bed. His ability to sustain laughter is seen in *A Night Out*, and Agee defines Chaplin's inflection through the example of *City Lights*. Lloyd's humiliating moments are explained in Agee's references to *Grandma's Boy* and *The Freshman*, while *Safety Last* illustrates the comedian's ability to thrill as well as amuse. The importance of Keaton's silly hat is discussed twice: once as the boat sinks and later as the actor madly races within a ferryboat wheel. The vividness of Agee's descriptions brings these examples to life.

2. Agee does with words what Lloyd did with gags. The first paragraphs set us up so that by paragraph 10, when the car collapses, we know exactly what he means by "topping a gag." Originally *The Freshman* contained a gag that got Lloyd "above" the audience, his initial refusal to lose the pants of his hastily basted-together suit. The example clearly explains why the actor's superior attitude

couldn't prevail, as the viewers' reactions during the trial run convinced Lloyd that not only the suit jacket but the pants had to slowly disintegrate in order to both milk and top the gag.

3. Keaton wasn't as popular as Chaplin (par. 3—'the greatest artist that ever lived') or Lloyd. In fact, "there are people who never much cared for Keaton" (par. 21). Agee naturally saves the least popular for last in this discussion of what made silent comedies great. "Even a smile was as deafeningly out of key as a yell" (par. 15). Without expression, his face "was irreducibly funny" (par. 16). The deadpan could convey a variety of mental states: "insanity," "imperturbability," "patience," and "endurance" (par. 17).

4. Because Agee is praising visual comedians, he gives the reader visual evidence of their talent. The "hair-raising illusion of noise" foreshadows the impact that noise (i.e., talking films) would have on the fate of silent screen stars.

5. Chaplin's drunken, unsteady movements are duplicated in the sentences of paragraphs 3 and 5, while Agee slowly unfolds the events of City Lights which are also slowly paced. The author's descriptions of Lloyd's Grandma's Boy (par. 8) and Safety Last (par. 9) are as scenic, rapid, and suspenseful as each film, while his discussion of Keaton's sinking with the boat is as understated as the actor's expression.

Language

2. Examples of metaphors include "soft-shoe dance" (par. 3), "poignant poetry" (par. 6), "uproarious Gethsemanes" (par. 8), "picture hangs thus by its eyelash" (par. 9), "the payoff of one gag sends him careening head downward through the abyss into another" (par. 11). Examples of similes include "Each new floor is like a new stanza in a poem" (par. 9); "his pictures are like a transcendent juggling act" (par. 15); "when he moved his eyes, it was like seeing them move in a statue" (par. 17); "...untouchable face—were as distinct and as soberly in order as an automatic gearshift" (par.

17).

3. "...the delicately weird mental processes of a man ethereally sozzled" (par. 3). "Each new floor is like a new stanza in a poem; and the higher and more horrifying it gets, the funnier it gets" (par. 9). "The last you see of him, the water lifts the hat off the stoic head and it floats away" (par. 16). Each sentence ends with a bang in duplication of the way these actors left their audiences. Any alteration in word order would have diminished the effect Agee was out to achieve.

APPEAL TO REASON:
DEDUCTIVE AND INDUCTIVE ARGUMENTS

THOMAS JEFFERSON, "The Declaration of Independence"
(pp. 340-345)

Content

1. Modern readers might not agree on what these "laws" are or whether they exist at all, but Jefferson's initial audience would have been used to hearing these terms. The 18th century was the time of a philosophical movement called "The Enlightenment," which, among other things, championed the idea of man having certain "natural rights" which could not be altered by any human being, and Jefferson's audience would probably have been very familiar with this idea. Thus, these terms are not defined and are sufficient support for later arguments. The allusion works well in light of the first sentence in paragraph 2: "All men are created equal," and all are entitled to "certain unalienable Rights."

2. Any government that overlooks or perverts the truths Jefferson has mentioned in the first sentence of this paragraph must be abolished and a new one created in its place. He presents this premise as a statement of fact rather than as an argument, and therefore he offers no proof. Sympathetic readers would have required no further proof, but to convince those who were less sympathetic, Jefferson catalogues Britain's offenses against the colonies. The list itself would seem to support the premise.

3. Many of the grievances involve the monarch's abuse of legal power (par. 3, 4, 5, 10). Such abuse threatened the colonists' liberty and happiness. Their lives were threatened by the actions mentioned in paragraph 8 (no protective government), paragraph 13 (establishment of hostile armies), paragraph 14 (giving the army superior protection and power), paragraph 16 (the quartering

of troops), and paragraph 17 (giving troops
immunity). Their livelihood--and therefore, one
means of the pursuit of happiness--was also
threatened by taxation (par. 18), the cutting off
of trade (par. 18), and acts of piracy and
destruction (par. 26).

4. Jefferson's ideal government would ensure the
"life, liberty, and pursuit of happiness" of its
citizens. Colonists, by their very nature, are
under the control of someone else and vulnerable to
unjust treatment. Only an independent nation could
be governed in this ideal manner.

5. The conclusion does evolve naturally from the
evidence and is even more convincing when he adds
that other steps, short of a show of force, had been
taken but failed to work (par. 30--"Our repeated
petitions have been answered only by repeated
injury"). When pleading didn't work and warnings
were ignored, separation seemed to the author to be
the only course left.

Strategies/Structures

1. The list grows in severity, with the king's least
serious offenses appearing first (par. 3--"He has
refused his Assent to Laws") and those directly
threatening the colonists' lives mentioned last
(par. 29--"He has excited domestic insurrections
amongst us.").

2. The Declaration was addressed to the king, its
initial audience, and to others in England less
well acquainted with the colonists' view of the
problems that had grown up between them and the
Crown. It is also a written vindication of the
colonists' actions and was intended for the
colonists as well, partly to move less zealous
citizens to take a stand. Finally, it was an
historical record which Jefferson was preparing for
future generations. It explained the factors which
led to the creation of a new government.

3. In paragraph 30, Jefferson explains how attempts at
peaceful solutions had not worked, and he labels
the king a tyrant. He then accuses the "British
brethren" (par. 31) who, like their leader, failed

to recognize or care about the colonists' mistreatment. Based on the severity of his accusations, it is unlikely that the British would have had a sudden change of heart and sided with the colonists. Essentially, it is a declaration of war.

Language

1. The tone is rational, matter-of-fact, and yet emphatic, critical, and determined. Jefferson probably didn't expect King George to be swayed, but the coolness of the tone might have at least made clear to the monarch what the consequences of his actions might be. The patriots would have been stirred by the cool recitation of their justifiable grievances; the wrongs are self-evident, however objectively stated.

MARTIN LUTHER KING, JR., "Letter from Birmingham Jail" (pp. 345-365)

Content

1. The first point in paragraph 4 is that all communities and states in America are interrelated. What concerns one location concerns all. Another assertion is that injustice anywhere in America should be of concern to all citizens since it diametrically opposes the idea of justice on which our government was formed. Finally, all Americans are part of the collective brotherhood and must concern themselves with the mistreatment of others of their number. King assumes that the self-evidence of these points is clear to all his readers, and so he doesn't provide additional "proof."

2. The justification--but not necessarily the proof--comes in paragraph 6, where King details the steps involved in nonviolent protests. All had been followed, but when they failed to yield positive results, there was "no alternative" except step four: civil disobedience. He needed to let his

audience know that all possible measures had been taken before the active protesting started. This information illustrates the protestors' willingness to achieve a peaceful solution. The statement is debatable to those having views that differ from King's, especially if they can think of other alternatives to civil disobedience that might accomplish the same ends.

3. The four-step plan includes the following: collecting proof of injustice, trying to negotiate with the opposition, undergoing "self-purification" through discussion and prayer, and finally, taking "direct action." As King explains in paragraph 8, the goal of direct action was to raise the "consciousness of the local and the national community" about the mistreatment of blacks, and they intended to use their "very bodies as a means of laying [their] case" before these onlookers.

4. First King is disappointed with the white moderates' acceptance of a "negative peace" (par. 23) that is unjust to so many. He's disappointed in their belief that problems will work themselves out in a "'more convenient season'"(par. 23). The moderate, in King's opinion, has become a slave to form, "order," and the status quo, all the while believing he's obeying the law (par. 24). King is disappointed that white churches have not supported his cause. Some have openly opposed it. While clergymen tell their parishoners that they should comply with desegregation laws, they are moved to do it by the laws of the courts rather than the laws of God. This is ironic considering the Christian message to love one's neighbor as oneself. King wants churches to "meet the challenge" and champion his cause (par. 44), even if this means non-conformity. King is advocating that Christians follow the example of their leader, Christ, also a nonconformist.

5. King refutes the argument by stating that people are wrong to assume that "time heals all wounds." He explains that people have this "strangely irrational notion that there is something in the very flow of time that will inevitably cure all ills" even though "time itself is neutral" (par. 26). He concludes by showing that men's "tireless efforts," not time's passage, have brought about positive change. King denies the charges that he

is an extremist by citing two extremes to his position: those who have acquiesced and lost their identity and those advocating immediate, violent action to bring about change. In light of these two extremes, King indeed seems a moderate.

Strategies/Structures

1. King explains in paragraph 1 that he is responding to the published condemnation by fellow pastors who took exception to his involvement in the demonstrations. The first sentence reveals his location ("...in the Birmingham Jail"). The salutation is addressed to his "Dear Fellow Clergymen," and he includes direct wording from their statement ("'...unwise and untimely'"). He appeals to their sense of reason at the end of the paragraph by saying, "I feel that you are men of genuine good will and that your criticisms are sincerely set forth."

2. The salutation and last sentence of paragraph 1 are addressed to eight ministers. So is his explanation in paragraph 2 of what brought him to Birmingham ("since you have been influenced..."). Again in paragraph 5 he addresses them directly ("But your statement..."). His final paragraph expresses his desire to meet them "as a fellow clergyman and a Christian brother," which shows King's desire for them to recognize their common bonds as humans, ministers, and Christians. The second audience consists of white moderates (white opponents wouldn't have read this and white supporters would have shared his views). This audience is revealed in paragraph 23 where he responds to moderates' complaints about his tactics. In paragraph 26 he responds to a specific moderate who has written to him. In paragraph 31 he reminds the moderates who regard him as an extremist that Jesus was "an extremist for love." King appeals to the moderates' sense of reason to win them over.

3. By citing theologians who represent three separate faiths to provide support of the belief that segregation is evil, King shows that this idea is important to members of all religions. Segregation isn't just a racial issue but a moral issue for all

believers of all faiths.

4. The argument changes from defensive to offensive in the second sentence of paragraph 23 where King states that he has "been gravely disappointed with the white moderates." Until this point he has justified his actions, but this marks the start of a counterattack.

5. King appeals to reason throughout most of the letter, and the change to an emotional appeal comes in paragraphs 27-30, where he describes the true extremists in the racial struggle and what bloody results might be expected if his course isn't given serious thought. He connects the two by showing how hard he's worked to keep the situation nonviolent and "reasonable," but if reason alone won't convince his readers, then he must move them emotionally by describing potential violence.

6. The answers to King's rhetorical questions are self-evident and illustrate most forcefully the injustice to which the blacks have been subjected.

Language

1. King defines a just law as "a man-made code that squares with the moral law or the law of God" while an unjust law is "out of harmony with the moral law" (par. 16). He further explains that all segregation laws "are unjust because segregation distorts the soul and damages the personality" (par. 16). This injustice is the springboard for his actions. The definitions clarify his motivation.

FRANCES FITZGERALD, "Ethnic Bias in Textbooks" (pp. 365-377)

Content

1. In the early nineteenth century the Spaniards were condemned for their "gold lust, cruelty to Indians, and crazed searchings for the Fountain of Youth" (par. 2). By the 1920's the image mellowed because

of acknowledgement of some of their contributions (par. 2--"Christianity, mission architecture, and domestic animals"), yet textbooks still noted that they "lacked 'moral and ethical character'" (par. 2). In the 60's, texts stressed the Spaniards' religious fervor and their desire for territorial monopoly. By the early 70's more emphasis was on contributions, "most of which are crops" (par. 2). In the mid-70's, texts broke with "the tradition of two centuries by making no reference to gold, slavery, or massacres of Indians" (par. 5). FitzGerald wanted to show how minimal these changes were, and they didn't always signal improvement. Although not explicitly stated, FitzGerald implies in paragraph 2 that the earlier textbook writing felt no need to be kind since "Spanish colonizers of the New World had always been American history's villains par excellence," and Hispanics were the "newest immigrant population" here; thus their late arrival could not have influenced what had been printed earlier.

2. Some books started including a little information on "large racial and ethnic groups" and lots of photographs, while a few included social history of these groups. Others dealt with the "'problems'" minority immigrants experienced here. There is still an imbalance in the coverage these groups receive (European ethnic groups receive more). Some publishers say little if anything about non-European minorities because they "are anxious not to offend" (par. 11). At best these attempts have resulted in a vague, inaccurate, or condescending presentation of information about minorities, especially non-European minorities.

3. Such photographs would only destroy the image textbook editors are trying to maintain about America, that our country is still the "land of opportunity," a melting pot where minorities will quickly be assimilated into mainstream culture and will fulfill "the American Dream." Sanitized photographs of smiling immigrants reinforce these cliché views.

4. The "majority" to whom these books are being sold might be offended to know that the minorities' reasons for "struggling" have actually come from those in the majority. While some books have attempted to be in part truthful and show what

steps have been taken to remedy the problem situations, they still don't explain what caused the problems in the first place, nor have they honestly revealed the failure of some of these reform programs.

5. From what FitzGerald says in paragraph 14, the ideal would be "a book that would include all these [social, cultural, ideologic] perspectives" or perhaps "different texts for the different sections of society." Her comments indicate "mass market" texts don't (and possibly can't) measure up to her ideal. The inquiry books are a better alternative perhaps, but they appeal to a very limited audience that is "largely white, upper middle class," and "extremely literate" (par. 15).

Strategies/Structures

1. The argument does grow more convincing as we see each step falling short of its mark. FitzGerald shows in each case how good intentions didn't produce the desired results.

2. All evidence does point to her final statement, but her thesis is clear from the first two sentences: history texts have overlooked and/or denigrated a large part of our population.

3. To a certain extent she does do the same thing. By citing specific books to give her argument its credibility, she has excluded others that might have weakened her case. The reader might well wonder if FitzGerald had indeed examined all history texts in preparation for writing this.

Language

2. Some words that reveal FitzGerald's position include: "little actual history" (par. 1), "served the newest immigrant population rather worse than it served any other group" (par. 2), "defamation of the Spanish character" (par. 2), "rewriting history backward to accommodate the new population" (par. 7), "brief dismissive passages about toiling masses" (par. 10). Her tone is subjective,

sarcastic, and critical as is seen in paragraph 1 ("The history texts have not actually found many women in America, but they have replaced their pictures of Dolley Madison with photographs of Susan B. Anthony"). Another example, in paragraph 11, is her discussion of the photographs of minorities included in textbooks ("The Puerto Ricans are smiling and healthy. The Chinese are smiling at healthy-looking vegetable stands"). She concludes by saying that it seems as if non-white Americans "tooks happy pills."

ANDREW HACKER, "E.R.A.--R.I.P." (pp. 377-385)

Content

1. Passage of the ERA initially seemed assured because its simple wording "summarized a principle accepted by the courts and embodied in legislation" (par. 3). Also, by the end of 1972, twenty-two of the thirty-eight needed states had ratified the amendment.

2. As people began to ascribe "concrete terms" to the amendment's rather general wording, its simplicity was viewed in a different light. One-time supporters feared the possible implications being discussed (in par. 8 Hacker mentions such issues as abortion and property rights pending divorce), and when militant feminists joined the cause, other supporters no longer wanted to share in their zeal for fear of guilt by association.

3. Since Hacker is most concerned here with explaining how and why women were divided on the ERA, his own feelings on the issue are understandably difficult to discern. He does a skillful job of showing why opponents felt threatened--in fact, nineteen of his thirty-two paragraphs are addressed to their objections--but at no point is it absolutely certain how he feels about the ERA. One clue, however, is given in the first paragraph ("few men cared much either way"), and the reader must wonder if Hacker is including himself in this number.

4. Hacker feels that housewives were most threatened, and he sees their complaints as being legitimate.

As he points out in the last paragraph, the
amendment ignored "the sensibilities of women not
avid for careers or for whom that option appears to
come too late," and "it jeopardized a way of life
they had entered in good faith" (par. 32).

5. As he points out is paragraph 1, "few men cared
much either way." Also, in paragraph 32 he
reiterates that it "was definitely a 'woman's
issue,' with women dominating both sides of the
struggle." These comments indicate Hacker's view
that men were apart from the issue. This is an
unsupported generalization and isn't justified in
view of the extensive public support of the ERA by
such highly visible men as President Jimmy Carter
and TV/film star Alan Alda, among others.

Strategies/Structures

1. In paragraph 15 he cites Friedan's figure of 17
percent of American households still adhering to
traditional structure (male as breadwinner, female
as homemaker), but he says this can be interpreted
another way. In paragraph 17 he maintains that
most women still hope to marry and have children
even if they do have jobs, and in paragraphs 18 and
19 he shows that statistics have been inaccurately
presented which place women who work only part-time
in the category of workers rather than homemakers.
In paragraph 27 he cites the statistic that only
one in three women over forty tends to remarry, but
he fails to account for the variables that have
contributed to this bit of information (e.g., for
many women this may be by choice). As the author
himself shows, numbers can be played with in
countless ways depending on what people are trying
to prove. He's trying to show how women should
still be considered homemakers even if they work
part-time, but an ERA supporter could use these
figures just as effectively to show that even
part-time female employees need the protection
offered by the amendment.

2. Hacker's original audience, Harper's readers,
typical of those favoring the ERA, would probably
have been convinced by his argument. Unconvinced
readers might have come from homemakers and other
groups that felt threatened by the ERA's allegedly

negative implications for members of that group (such as the presumed ease of divorce under ERA (par. 20-24), the alleged disappearance of alimony (par. 21), and the sexual threat of employed women to their married male co-workers (par. 25-27)).

Language

1. Hacker seems to feel that the amendment's chances for ratification ended as soon as its threat to the status quo was made known (par. 7).

2. An objective tone is desirable because it forces readers to read very carefully in order to determine what the writer is advocating. It's less likely that a hostile audience will be immediately antagonized if the writer is objective. There are a few instances where Hacker's objectivity lags. Sarcasm appears in paragraph 9 where he says, "Nor could its supporters imagine how any rational woman could object to these goals," and in paragraph 11 where he points out, "nor was it legitimate to settle for being a secretary or a stewardess." While these two instances point to the singlemindedness of ERA supporters, Hacker also ridicules ERA opponents in paragraph 22: "...nor does she even wish to contemplate how she would survive were that situation [divorce] ever to come about." The sarcasm in these instances only supports his point that women themselves were so divided that the amendment failed.

APPEAL TO EMOTIONS AND ETHICS

GEORGE ORWELL, "Marrakech" (pp. 388-430)

Content

1. Orwell's implicit thesis is that colonial empires are dehumanizing and inhumane. As he points out in paragraph 3, "it is always difficult to believe that you are walking among human beings. All colonial empires are in reality founded upon that fact."

2. Orwell restricts himself to a discussion of one colonial government situation, but readers can easily see how his thesis might apply in any area where one group, for its own self-interest, subverts the interests and well-being of another group. While his example is limited, his thesis isn't.

3. The most apparent value is that all people are entitled to their dignity as humans (par. 3--"Are they really the same flesh as yourself?"). His examples imply another value: that colonial governments are obligated to ensure the basics of life (food, shelter, sanitation, and health protection) to those they govern. Finally, he values the inhabitants' right to rebel when they aren't adequately provided for. His readers aren't likely to share his views because he is writing for supporters of colonial rule. Orwell must try to convince his readers as he moves through the essay.

4. His examples show that poverty and powerlessness go hand in hand. Without resources, the people must remain dependent on their colonial rulers for everything. The marching soldiers are a warning. Orwell indicates that at some point the oppressed will surely rise up against their oppressors (par. 26--"'How much longer can we go on kidding these people? How long before they turn their guns in the other direction?'"). The troops are an unhappy yet powerful reminder of what will happen should

mistreatment of natives by colonial governments persist. This is a variation on the point that Orwell makes in "Shooting an Elephant": "When white man turns tyrant it is his own freedom that he destroys."

Strategies/Structures

1. The startling one-sentence paragraph immediately gains the reader's attention and compels him to continue reading. Its vividness and incompleteness cause readers to ask questions: Whose corpse? Which restaurant? Who's narrating? Why did the flies return?

2. Although the beginning is hardly aesthetically appealing, it appeals to readers' curiosity about the grotesque, much as traffic accidents draw the attention of passing motorists. Orwell seems to know this dark side of human nature, and in keeping with the unpleasantness of his subject, he begins with an unpleasant description that sets the stage. The colonial governments turn countries' inhabitants into little more than walking corpses. In the eyes of the rulers, these people are not humans like themselves. Orwell's use of such details as flies, corpses, and gravesites strengthens his point that colonial governments are guilty of figurative, if not literal, genocide.

3. Orwell begins with the corpses (par. 1) and moves toward the final example of armed marching troops (par. 27) to illustrate his belief that oppressed people can and will rise up in rebellion. He devotes the most space to examples that illustrate the deplorable conditions of the natives in life and death (par. 2--their pitiful burial sites; par. 9--the filthy Jewish quarter; par. 19--the impossible farming attempts; par. 20--the mistreatment of old women; par. 21--the brutality to animals). The amount of development in these instances gives impetus to his point that there is just cause for rebellion. Orwell uses visual examples to let us literally (visually) and figuratively (intellectually, emotionally) "see" the problems in Marrakech.

4. Orwell seems to be addressing himself particularly

to a white, economically advantaged audience that
either supports colonial rule or does nothing to
stop its existence. This is most evident in
paragraph 26: "But there is one thought which
every white man (and in this connection it doesn't
matter twopence if he calls himself a Socialist)
thinks when he sees a black army marching past."
Others are excluded from his audience, since they
are the oppressed, not the oppressors.

Language

1. Orwell's implied definition is found in paragraph
   3, where he describes "two hundred thousand
   inhabitants, of whom at least twenty thousand own
   literally nothing except the rags they stand up
   in." Each example supports this statement: in
   par. 2--no coffins for burials; in par. 8--no food
   for "an employee of the Municipality;" in par.
   11--the luxury of his handout cigarettes; in par.
   17--no farm tools; in par. 20--no carts for hauling
   wood, and no money.

2. Orwell's seemingly objective, reportorial tone
   allows the readers' reactions to be emotionally
   charged. His tone reflects the callous attitude of
   those in power, and, through a series of negative
   examples, he wants his audience to recognize how
   inappropriate and inhuman this attitude truly is.

JONATHAN SWIFT, "A Modest Proposal"   (pp. 399-409)

Content

1. Swift's overt and implied theses are the same:
   there is a workable solution to Ireland's economic
   problems. The solutions, however, are quite
   different. While the narrator suggests a gruesome
   plan for economic recovery (marketing the children
   of Ireland's poor), Swift's implied solutions (found
   in par. 29) depend on sensible, human measures that
   would only benefit those the narrator ostensibly
   seeks to exploit.

2. The narrator ostensibly seeks to define his "fair,

cheap, and easy method of making these [Irish Catholic] children sound, useful members of the commonwealth" (par. 2). He pretends to value the welfare of the children's parents and the country's economy above all else. The economic advantages of the plan include the creation of a new national dish (par. 9), a way for tenants to adequately repay their landlords (par. 12), a reduction in the number of Ireland's Catholics (par. 13), an incentive for landlords to be kinder to their tenants (par. 14), an increase in the production of gloves and shoes (par. 15), and the development of new jobs to accommodate the growing demand for edible children (par. 16). Swift is concerned about the lives these poor children can expect to lead in light of their poverty and an indifferent government.

3. The list indicates that Ireland was overpopulated (par. 21), it was torn from disagreements over religious and political ideology (par. 21), and its tenant farmers were the victims of exploitation by their absentee landlords (par. 22). Ireland's wealth was being spent on imported goods (par. 23), and its citizens couldn't afford to support their children (par. 24). Finally, there was a problem with out-of-wedlock births and cruel treatment of children by parents and of wives by their husbands (par. 26).

4. At the time Swift was writing, America was still a complex of British colonies, and it was considered a savage land filled with equally savage inhabitants. What information Britain did receive of the New World was often uncomplimentary or inaccurate because America, an unsettled land, was being compared to an old established nation. Those who had chosen to move to America were religious malcontents, fortune hunters, debtors—in short, European misfits—and for this reason the narrator claims the idea originally came from one such barbarian. (Students' attention might well be directed to Ebenezer Cooke's satiric poem "The Sot-Weed Factor," written in 1708, for another British writer's damning assessment of the colonists.)

5. The response Swift wanted from his audience was a demand for immediate correction of this problem by the government, and correction that would not

threaten the well-being of any segment of the population. He also wanted the suggestions listed in paragraph 29 to be viewed as earnest proposals worth consideration.

Strategies/Structures

1. Swift's narrator is the rational logician who lacks any shred of human compassion or concern for the welfare of others. He denies emotional attachments people might have to anything other than the economic soundness of the state. His ostensible attitude parallels that of the indifferent government. The overt proposal is too outrageous to be taken seriously, as readers of good will have only to realize by testing it against their common-sense understanding of what is ethically right and wrong. Also, the narrator's protests about trying sensible solutions in paragraph 29 are obviously intended to discredit the narrator.

2. The statistics lend credibility to the narrator's argument. He has the facts and figures to support his proposal. The numbers themselves are as coldly impersonal as the narrator who uses them. He doesn't view people as individuals, just as items in the grand scheme of the country's economy.

3. The indirect approach is less offensive to readers who might have disregarded or been offended by an overt attack on the problems arising from their governing policies. By using this tactic Swift allows the audience to at first be outraged by the exaggerated proposal so that they will ultimately realize a sensible solution is well within their grasp. The indirect approach frees the writer from responsibility for what the narrator says. Also, it allows readers to see the error of their ways without the author having to preach to them directly. Hopefully his exaggerations will move his readers to action. The disadvantages of such an approach include the risk of misinterpretation by the readers. While some might be merely amused by such a ludicrous idea, others might take Swift literally and completely miss the point. Those offended by the literal reading would view the situation of a depressed and debased Ireland with all its problems as preferable to a cannibalistic

country.

Language

1. While the narrator seems sincere and rational (he professes in the first sentence that "It is a melancholy object..."), the essay's tone is sarcastic and ironic. Consequently, we are suspicious and doubtful of the narrator's altruism and good intentions. None of his overt suggestions can be taken seriously. While the sarcasm undercuts the narrator's thoughts, it serves to clarify Swift's implied claim that there is a sound solution to Ireland's problem.

2. The reference to "a child just dropped from its dam," and other animalistic imagery, shows the narrator's insensitivity to the poor and the way they must live. To him these people aren't really humans, but are just like other living things that procreate but have no attachments to their offspring. The narrator also refers to wives as "breeders" (par. 16) and compares human breeders and livestock (par. 10). He suggests that cooks prepare children as though they were "roasting pigs" (par. 16).

3. In paragraph 21 the narrator says the country is "yearly overrun" with Catholics because they are the "principal breeders" and the cause of the country's overpopulation. Also, they are "our most dangerous enemies" because they don't support the kingdom's ruling monarch. These clues let us know the term is not complimentary. The term shows how little the Anglican government cared about its Catholic citizens.

MAX SHULMAN, "Love Is a Fallacy"   (pp. 409-422)

Content

1. <u>Dicto Simpliciter</u>: An all-encompassing generality that overlooks exceptions to the rule (Jogging promotes fitness. Therefore everyone should jog.). <u>Hasty Generalization</u>: A conclusion based on too

little information (Sam, José, and Beauregard are happy freshmen. All freshmen are happy.). <u>Post Hoc</u>: The inaccurate citing of a cause for an unrelated effect (After every visit to my doctor, I get ill). <u>Contradictory Premises</u>: Facts of an argument that cancel each other out, thereby negating the argument ("Catch 22": To get out of military duty, one must be crazy, but since no sane person would want to serve, everyone who wanted out was, by definition, sane). <u>Ad Misericordiam</u>: Bypassing a question's answer by trying to evoke the questioner's sympathy (Do you have your homework? Answer: I was at home last night when the house caught fire, I lost everything, and I had to stay at the Y where my clothes were stolen.). <u>False Analogy</u>: Incorrectly comparing one thing to another that has nothing in common with it (Why live with someone before marriage? Answer: You don't buy a pair of shoes without first trying them on). <u>Hypothesis Contrary to Fact</u>: Drawing a conclusion from an unfounded assumption (If the English hadn't settled in the New World, America would still be an Indian nation). <u>Poisoning the Well</u>: Discrediting an opponent by attacking his character (Mayor Brown was seen in the company of gamblers, so we can't believe his sincerity about wanting to help the needy).

2. Petey thinks it will, but this is a <u>Post Hoc</u> fallacy. The coat (cause) doesn't turn someone into a celebrity (effect). Other factors contribute to this distinction. He has seen the Big Men on Campus wearing such coats and assumes this is all he needs to be one. He overlooks their personalities, financial status, looks, intellect, charm, etc. With other attributes, Petey could be a Big Man on Campus without the coat.

3. No, Dobie's assumption is inaccurate. Intelligence involves more than logic. In his relationship with Polly he makes a hasty generalization (in par. 21--succesful lawyers had wives who were "beautiful, gracious, intelligent women," and he, too, would be successful if he had such a wife). This assumption might also be labeled <u>dicto simpliciter</u> or <u>post hoc</u> as well.

4. Shulman has used stereotypes as characters because he can count on his readers to recognize the types and to laugh at the parodies of their thinking

(par.1--"Cool was I and logical"), their language
(par. 60--"Oo, terrif'"), their appearance (par.
54--"He looked like a mound of dead raccoons"), and
thir behavior (par. 47--"He just stood and stared
with mad lust at the coat"). Polly is smarter than
Dobie imagines, and so is Petey. They get what they
want by playing along with Dobie's rules. He,
ultimately, is the loser.

Strategies/Structures

1. Dobie is to be laughed at. The joke is on him, and we delight in his reward. It is a humorous essay, and Dobie is the source of our laughter. People continue reading to see if he will get what he deserves and because of the fun of Shulman's delivery.

2. Humor is appropriate because it makes the subject memorable. Each fallacy, when linked with a humorous example, will be remembered vividly. While the definitions might not be as detailed as they might be in a logic text, the reader knows Shulman's purpose is more to entertain than to instruct.

3. The outcome is predictable. This ridiculous character, whose pride is insufferable, must get his inevitable comeuppance at the hands of those he intended to exploit.

Language

1. Polly's speech is characterized by abbreviations of adjectives (par. 57--"delish," "marvy," "sensaysh"). She is also quick to show her enthusiasm by using exclamations such as "Oo" (par. 60) and "Wow-dow" (par. 65). She also has difficulty finding exactly the right words to express what she means (par. 69--"I mean it builds the body and everything"). In general these speech traits help Shulman characterize Polly as the airhead Dobie imagines her to be. Dobie's speech, however, is arrogant (par. 1--"Keen, calculating, perspicacious, acute, and astute--I was all of these"), condescending (par. 2--"Same age, same background, but dumb as an ox"), and downright

stuffy (par. 2---"To be swept up in every new craze that comes along, to surrender yourself to idiocy just because everybody else is doing it---this, to me, is the acme of mindlessness"). His dialogue serves to reveal his separateness from his friends and reinforces the manipulative aspect of his character.

2. Polly's language is a parody of that associated with flighty coeds more intent on having a good time than getting an education. Upon reading her slangy expressions, readers might at first see her as the dumb creature Dobie described, but by the end we realize that she deserves more credit. Her counterpart, Petey, also uses language intended to ridicule males of the same ilk. Like Polly, he incorporates a good bit of slang into his speech and tends to become melodramatic over minor issues. Again, the reader at first believes Petey to be shallow, insincere, and vapid, but by the end we realize he isn't as dumb as he seemed at first. Just the opposite is true in Dobie's case. Throughout the essay his speech seems to be that of the intellectual, yet in light of the outcome we see the language belied true intelligence. His inflated language is also a means of self-deception.

RICHARD RODRIGUEZ, "None of This Is Fair" (pp. 422-428)

Content

1. Rodriguez explains in paragraph 20 that "Affirmative Action programs are unfair to white students," but what is most unfair is the government's ignoring of "the most seriously disadvantaged" (par. 20) regardless of their race.

2. Affirmative Action refers to programs mandated by law to ensure equal educational and career oportunities for equally qualified U.S. citizens, regardless of their sex, race, or ethnic background. Reverse discrimination involves active recruitment of those in a minority while overlooking those in the majority, ostensibly for the purpose of creating racial or sexual balance in a given setting. Compared to his colleagues at

Berkeley, Rodriguez's experiences in finding a job reveal that Affirmative Action programs (from which he benefited) were actually leading to cases of reverse discrimination. He shows the causal relationship between the two.

3. Rodriguez does expect his audience to generalize. Not just one university wanted him; several actively sought him out but ignored his equally well qualified white classmates. We can assume that if he received numerous teaching offers, then well-qualified minorities seeking positions in other areas must have also been shown preferential treatment.

4. Those presently receiving the benefits of Affirmative Action programs are minorities who are educated and not so indigent that their dreams of success have disappeared. Reverse discrimination victims include whites with good education and ability and expectations that their training and abilities will be appropriately rewarded who are bypassed for jobs because they are in the majority.

5. Those most in need of Affirmative Action programs are the "silent" minorities who "lack the confidence and skills a good primary and secondary education provides" (par. 20). Rodriguez waits until paragraph 20 in order to leave the reader with the main point he has been leading up to. He has explained his benefits as a recipient of Affirmative Action and his colleagues' unfair treatment, but he ends by clarifying that neither of these sides should be the subjects of this "debate" (par. 20). The ones who really need Affirmative Action's advantages aren't even present in the discussion. He dramatically leaves them out until the last moment because they in reality are the ones who have been left out. They are the ones who don't even realize that they have the right to want something more from life than poverty.

Strategies/Structures

1. While Rodriguez's guilt and hypocrisy make him unattractive to himself, his honesty is appealing to readers. Despite his admitted flaws, he is perceived as a concerned, sensitive individual

whose views are understandable and convincing. With this kind of candid presentation, Rodriguez can win the audience to his side, and this is the ultimate aim of any writer of an argument.

2. No specific example is given because Rodriguez is bringing home his point about their invisibility and silence. He's talking about the desperately impoverished of any race, "white, black, brown" (par. 20).

Language

1. The indirect discourse sets the stage for Rodriguez's ultimate realization that Affirmative Action programs are "misdirected" (par. 20). Before the conversation with this Berkeley classmate, which is presented as direct discourse, Rodriguez had not been moved to act against the opportunities Affirmative Action had provided for him. This episode signals a turning point and is emphasized by the author's change in language usage. Had he not made this change, the importance of this event would have lost its force.

2. The simile explains both the writer's and the audience's "distance" from those truly in need of help. The hopeless poor, like boys on the overpasses, are seen from afar but are quickly put out of the driver's mind because they live "in some other part of town." The figure of speech has a long-lasting effect. By comparing one thing (uneducated poor) to something more familiar to the reader (boys on an overpass), the writer creates a vivid connection that perhaps will be recalled each time the reader sees the familiar half of the comparison.

REVISING AND EDITING

DONALD M. MURRAY, "The Maker's Eye: Revising Your Own Manuscripts" (pp. 434-445)

Content

1. Although it is dangerous to try to separate thinking and writing--since every revision in writing might indicate one in the writer's thinking--in Murray's view the first draft should be almost totally concerned with thinking out what we have to say. Only after we've expressed the basic ideas can we begin the real process of writing--determining how to best say what we've thought. Whether or not Murray's essay can convince people that they should revise, it is almost impossible to argue about one point: many professional writers think revision is essential.

2. The trick is that good writing needs to seem fresh and spontaneous--and so needs to be created in passion--yet, a writer must also be able to separate the good from the bad, to judge between those products of passion that work and those that don't. That judgment requires a certain coldness, an intellectual approach to a work that may have been initially written with emotion. Thus a writer must be both artist and critic, producing the work from the inside and revising it from the outside. Since most of us cannot do both at once, we separate the tasks in time. Ideally, implies Ciardi, we create the drafts in passion, we wait, and then we return in cold detachment to revise.

3. Murray's list can be divided into three categories: content (information, meaning, and audience), form (form, structure, development, and dimension), and style (voice). Those are the components of good writing, so the list is both realistic and comprehensive.

4. Murray's assertion that the "maker's eye" will have an accurate perception of these stylistic needs seems to rest on an optimistic assumption that

there is an almost inherent beauty to verbal art to which writers naturally respond. Perhaps he is a bit too optimistic: our responses to all the arts are more culturally conditioned than that. Perhaps the only way to develop a feeling for what good prose should sound like is the time-consuming process of reading a great deal of what our culture deems good writing. No one, including Murray, can provide a checklist that can allow us to fully judge our own work.

Strategies/Structures

1. Murray has reduced the sentence in successive revisions from eight words to five words to three words without loss of meaning. Indeed, the meaning of "Rewriting isn't virtuous" is more poised and emphatic than in the two earlier revisions. Contemporary taste in style encourages conciseness; Word Watchers--experts on style, editors, teachers--like Weight Watchers, recommend aiming for a trim, lean body of prose that can function efficiently and effectively without laboring under the burden of extra words.

2. The original paragraph 8 seems directed towards writers in general, while the new paragraph 8 clarifies the audience and so clarifies the point: "Hey, students, if you think your writing is no good, don't worry--professional writers go through that, too." The central idea--the call for confidence--is salvaged and tailored for a slightly different audience.

    Analogies, comparisons of one thing to another, are useful only when the audience knows one term of the comparison much better than they know the other: if your audience doesn't know anything about racquetball but does know something about tennis and handball, comparison and contrast can be useful. If they already know how to play racquetball, they'll think you've underestimated their knowledge if you try to explain the game in terms of tennis and handball.

    Since Murray's revised article is intended for students, who are presumably less sophisticated than his original audience of professional or semi-professional writers, it's pointless to try to explain writing to them in terms they probably don't know any better than the terms of writing. Since Murray evidently assumed that student readers wouldn't understand or respond to the simile of "battered old hive," he dropped it.

The longer versions contain more real information and so are better.

Language

1. Murray, responding to the women's movement that grew between 1973, the date of his first published version, and 1980, the date of his second version, is trying to avoid the inherent sexism of the English language: "they" is more inclusive than "he," both because it is neutral in gender and because it is plural rather than singular.

2. The revision is better because it focuses on how a writer is like any other craftsman and on what he must do as a craftsman. We are not distracted by unnecessary references to clanking motors (see answer to Strategies/Structures #2 above).

3. The original version of the article was published in The Writer, and was so intended for The Writer's audience, people who would like to publish professionally or who are already doing so. By changing "the beginning writer" to "students" in the first sentence, Murray has shifted his audience and therefore his purpose as well. The article is now intended to demonstrate to students that their anxieties are shared by professional writers and that their need to revise is the same as the professionals'.

LINDA PETERSON, "From Egocentric Speech to Public Discourse: Richard Wright Composes His Thoughts on Black Boy" (pp. 445-463)

Content

1. It is easy enough to infer the contents of Black Boy. Wright tells us that he grew up in the South;

he tells us in both versions that the southern environment was "bleak, prejudice-ridden"; and he praises a number of books for their honest images of people trying to live in a bleak, hostile environment. Black Boy is an honest account of a black boy in a hostile environment.

2. Peterson tells us that in his first draft Wright used something of a "jot list" and then proceeded to a loosely-organized, narrative-style "focused free-writing" (Elbow's terms). These egocentric, autobiographical--and process-oriented ("How I did it"; "How I reached these conclusions")--versions are common to the first drafts of many good writers.

3. Wright revised his essay so that it would appeal to readers whose experiences might be very different from his own. The focus changed from the process of how he made his decision to write Black Boy (version 1) to the consequences of that decision (final version)--the resulting universality of the novel. This distancing of the essay from himself took considerable effort because the autobiographical contents of Black Boy and the subject of oppression are obviously very important--and very emotional--for Wright.

4. Wright's changing sense of audience is reflected in the ending of each draft. Both drafts conclude with the same assertion--that "the Negroes in America have a duty far beyond themselves in reminding the nation of their plight." However, in the first draft, Wright does not explain how a non-black audience could respond positively to this "reminding." Quite possibly, as Peterson suggests, this is because in the original draft Wright imagined a hostile white audience that would not respond positively. By the time he wrote the more public draft, however, he could imagine a more sympathetic audience, and so he offers an explanation of how they might be able to respond positively.

Strategies/Structures

1. a) He eliminates personal references that would make sense only to him ("That sense came slowly,

bit by bit..." (par. 2)).
   b) He eliminates the repetition of the assertion, "I had a chance to grasp the meaning of phases of my own environment by looking at them through the eyes of an alien artist" (second draft, par. 5).
   c) The most obvious elimination of a phrase that emphasizes the differences between a possible white audience and Wright is in paragraph 5: "what would sound very strange to many whites..." Wright still recognizes the differences, however, and he calls attention to them in his next to last paragraph ("the experiences are alien to the sons and daughters of America's middle class families").
   d) Wright uses the first person throughout, but his most powerful use of his personal voice is in the last paragraph of the final draft. Here he speaks directly to us, from a position of wisdom and knowledge: "I know...." He openly states his own position: "I feel that...." Finally, he reminds us of what we should do: "And when you hear...remember that...." That's more than simple disclosure; it's the voice of a real person speaking to us.

2. Wright gains a great deal of strength and power by shortening his essay. In condensing an essay, however, a writer must be careful not to lose anything essential. Most of the bulk Wright cuts is information about the four autobiographies he mentions and his attempt to address white Americans in paragraph 9. Since Wright himself admits that he didn't have any of the four books in mind when he wrote Black Boy and, since paragraph 9 is, as Peterson points out, a "false start," both passages can be judged extraneous and eliminated. Nothing essential has been lost.

3. As Peterson points out, the first paragraph of the first draft projects a defiant, almost hostile Wright: "We can almost feel his fists clenched." By the end of the final version, however, he seems magnanimous, and more powerful, as he invites all readers into the chorus of voices calling for freedom. He is altogether more engaging, which is what he wants to be.
   Peterson--without openly asserting her own personality--assumes a position of total knowledge. For example, in paragraph 2, she begins, "We know" (notice, not "I know"); continues with "No doubt"; and proceeds to

tell us exactly what Wright wants to do, what
he actually did as he wrote, and how an expert
in the field (Linda Flower) would explain what
he did. This confident stance causes us to
trust her and believe her analysis.

Language

1. Peterson gives Flower's definition of egocentric
   speech in paragraph 7, but her own explanation in
   paragraph 5 is perhaps clearer: in the first
   draft, "Wright is literally talking to himself,"
   thinking out loud without concern for how it will
   sound to others. Moving to "public discourse," a
   medium in which we can all meet, requires that
   Wright not only find a "common ground" of
   experience and philosophy, but also that he craft a
   rhetorical structure that will draw us to that
   common ground. Public discourse—open
   communication—thus requires both a content and a
   style that are accessible to the general public.

2. In choice of vocabulary and image, and in some
   general aspects of style, Peterson's writing merges
   nicely with Wright's. Both essays are
   straightforward; the vocabulary of each is fairly
   simple and the sentences are not overly long. The
   most obvious difference between the two styles is
   that Peterson does not project the strong personal
   voice that Wright projects; she has chosen to
   subordinate her voice to his. By doing this, she
   successfully focuses the attention of her readers
   on Wright and what he is doing. This is
   appropriate to her purpose—she is trying to be
   informative, trying to teach us the craft of
   revision. Her personality is not the issue.
   Wright's purpose—to explain himself and challenge
   his readers to recognize him—requires the stronger
   voice that he projects.

WILLIAM ZINSSER, "Style"   (pp. 463-470)

Content

1. Zinsser sees style as the projection of a writer's

personality through his words. It seems very close to what Peter Elbow refers to as "voice" (pp. 18-21). A natural voice should produce the freshness and spontaneity that Murray calls for. Yet Zinsser and Murray emphasize different ways of developing style. Murray, writing on revision, emphasizes the detachment and craftsmanship necessary to achieve the appearance of spontaneity; Zinsser, even though he, too, uses a metaphor from carpentry, emphasizes the psychological and personal demands of writing with conviction.

2. If style comes from the personality of the writer, it cannot be learned--although it certainly can be developed by each individual. When we compare works by Hemingway and Fitzgerald, we don't get the sense of two craftsmen using a different set of literary tricks; we get the sense of two very different personalities. Favorite writers can be identified by style.

3. Zinsser uses this expression to point to the self-consciousness of most writing: writers often set out with an idea of what they should sound like, so they end up sounding not like themselves, but like some artificial ideal. For Zinsser, that's bound to produce a piece of writing that is phony and bad.

4. Writing in the first person makes it easier to be ourselves and express our own opinions instead of trying to sound like someone else or express the opinions we think we should have. If we practice writing in the first person, some of our own style will come through even when we're forced to use third person constructions. Although it is true that many newspapers, magazines, and teachers still do not allow the use of the first person, more and more are allowing it. Even the style manual of the American Psychological Association authorizes such usage in its professional journals. The first person is appropriate whenever someone has asked for your opinion--at work, at school, among friends, and in many instances where your opinion is identified as your personal, perhaps idiosyncratic, view.

Strategies/Structures

1. Zinsser's style certainly seems all these things; it's certainly unaffected. Most readers probably wouldn't expect a Yale professor to begin an essay on style by talking about "bloated monsters that lie in ambush." That's not stuffy writing. Whether it's personable or not is probably a matter of whether the reader responds favorably to Zinsser's authorial persona.

2. It reflects Zinsser's idea of what good style is. To Zinsser, a sense of the first person is absolutely essential to good style--even if the "first person" isn't actually used. If he's right, it would be hard to over-emphasize the importance of the first person.

Language

1. The analogy to carpentry sounds good, and it seems accurate. You do need to know the basic skills of a craft before you go on to the fine points. However, the discussion might not be particularly appropriate to Zinsser's point; the "style" of a piece of furniture is NOT recognized as the product of a carpenter's personality. It is recognized by its similarities to other examples of the style. True, carpenters differ in skill, and there are good and not-so-good Chippendale pieces, but there is a set of characteristics which define a piece as a Chippendale. The comparison to the wearing of a toupée seems closer to Zinsser's main point: you should look like yourself, and you should write like yourself. Writing is much more individualistic than we usually think of carpentry as being.

2. Zinsser promises that writing in the first person will make writing seem more natural, more relaxed, and more personal, and it will relay a clearer sense of a writer's personal convictions. Zinsser's essay seems to do all of these things; it's certainly relaxed and casual, and whether we like him or not, whether we agree with him or not, his essay certainly seems to give us a clear indication of him and his opinion.

3. Zinsser comes across as relaxed, informal, fair-minded (par. 3), and self-confident--perhaps to the point of arrogance. Some people might be put off by a professor telling us "Few people realize how badly they write" (par. 5). Some of his images might seem distasteful to some people: we have "bloated monsters that lie in ambush" (par. 1), a writer that is "like a man...being prodded for a possible hernia" (par. 13), and a question: "What can be done to put the writer out of these miseries?" (par. 14). When a writer projects as much personality as Zinsser, he does run the risk that people won't particularly care for the personality he projects.

ANGELA BOWMAN, "Freddie the Fox and My Fifth Christmas" (pp. 470-474)

Content

1. Freddie the Fox represents a number of things for Bowman, but the most important thing he represents is her independence of mind. In the first version, that thesis becomes clear only in the last sentence. In the revision, the thesis is clear at the end of paragraph 1.

2. Literally, the connection of Freddie to the growing independence of Bowman's mind is that the stuffed animal was present at two significant times when Angela was forced to realize that she couldn't simply accept everything she was told. His symbolic importance to her is made most clear in the last paragraph of the second version. The underlying symbolic implication is never directly stated: an independent mind is "clever, like a fox," and as free as a wild animal that must live by its wits.

3. In the first version we might guess from the second paragraph that Angela is black (although it isn't absolutely clear). In the revision, it is clear from the first paragraph. Because this essay concerns Bowman's acceptance of her racial identity and ultimate pride in it, it is appropriate to indicate her race early in the discussion.

Strategies/Structures

1. The most important revisions are those in the first paragraph. In the first version, Bowman begins with a false start about her stuffed animal collection. Only gradually does she begin to focus on Freddie: she asserts late in the paragraph that Freddie helps her to remember her fifth Christmas, but she doesn't clarify what the significance of that Christmas was. In the second version, she begins immediately with Freddie, announces his importance, and, in doing so, outlines the course her paper will take.

2. There are two kinds of repetitions in the first version. In the first paragraph, there are a number of sentences that repeat the same information: "It was a confusing time....I did not understand what he was talking about....It was confusing for me." This kind of repetition is common in rough drafts and can easily be remedied by eliminating some of the sentences. The other kind of repetition is a little more complicated: in paragraph 3, Bowman back-tracks and repeats much of the earlier information. Faulty organization is the problem here; the more thoughtful, directed organization of the second version eliminates the problem.

3. In the revision, the references to Freddie occur in the opening and closing paragraphs. In this final version, these references give Freddie his proper place: he is a symbol of the more important events that are described between the opening and the closing. In the rough draft, the references to Freddie at the beginning of each paragraph give an artifical sense of unity to the draft. When the organization of a paper is truly sound—as it is in the second version—a writer doesn't need to resort to linguistic tricks like unnecessary repetition.

4. Each of the first three paragraphs begins in the past—during Bowman's fifth Christmas—and proceeds to her present reflections on those past experiences. The fourth paragraph concludes the process: it is entirely a present reflection on the past. The last paragraph is a coda that

succinctly states the idea that past and present are linked. This principle of organization does lie beneath the surface of the first draft, but the second version makes it clear.

Language

1. The vocabulary of the revision is not exotic or unusually sophisticated; it is better because it is much more accurate. Bowman names her feeling about her race: pride. She names the personal quality she wants: independence of mind. With an aptly-worded contrast, she describes her feelings toward Christmas: "flesh and blood Santa Claus" vs "true spirit of Christmas, generous and loving."

2. By eliminating repetitions (Strategies/Structures, answer 2) and choosing more exact words (above), Bowman is able to say much more with fewer words.

The Essay Connection: Readings for Writers

TOPICAL TABLE OF CONTENTS

(page numbers refer to pages in the text)

Topics

1. On Writing and Revising

Joan Didion, "On Keeping a Notebook"	4-13
Woody Allen, "Selections from the Allen Notebooks"	13-18
Peter Elbow, "Freewriting"	18-22
Linda Flower, "Writing for an Audience"	238-243
Donald Murray, "The Maker's Eye: Revising Your Own Manuscripts" (multiple drafts)	434-445
Linda Peterson, "Richard Wright Composes His Thoughts on *Black Boy*"	445-463
William Zinsser, "Style"	463-470

2. People and Portraits

Studs Terkel, "John Fuller, Mail Carrier"	23-28
John Leonard, "The Only Child"	28-32
Frederick Douglass, "Resurrection"	57-63
N. Scott Momaday, "A Kiowa Grandmother"	172-179
Judy Syfers, "I Want a Wife"	206-209
Barry Lopez, "My Horse"	305-313
Bruce Catton, "Grant and Lee"	313-319
Suzanne Britt Jordan, "That Lean and Hungry Look"	319-323

3. The Natural World

E.B. White, "Once More to the Lake"	39-47
Tim Payne, "Bar Harbor, Maine"	75-79
Rachel Carson, "The Grey Beginnings"	97-109
Annie Dillard, "Transfiguration"	180-184
Hans C. von Baeyer, "The Wonder of Gravity"	210-220
Loren Eiseley, "The Brown Wasps"	272-281
Carl Sagan, "The Cosmic Calendar"	289-295

4. **Scientists at Work**

Berton Roueché, "The Neutral Spirit: A Portrait of Alcohol"	91-97
Lewis Thomas, "On Magic and Medicine"	130-136
Robert Jastrow, "Man of Wisdom"	136-142
Hans C. von Baeyer, "The Wonder of Gravity"	210-220
Lewis Thomas, "The Technology of Medicine"	243-250

5. **Places**

E.B. White, "Once More to the Lake"	39-47
Natalie Crouter, "Release from Captivity"	69-75
Tim Payne, "Bar Harbor, Maine"	75-79
Mark Twain, "Uncle John's Farm"	155-162
John McPhee, "The Pine Barrens"	163-171
Kristin King, "Ontonagon"	185-187
Joan Didion, "Marrying Absurd"	268-272
Loren Eiseley, "The Brown Wasps"	272-281
George Orwell, "Marrakech"	388-399
Jonathan Swift, "A Modest Proposal"	399-409

6. **Families**

John Leonard, "The Only Child"	28-32
E.B. White, "Once More to the Lake"	39-47
Ann Upperco, "Learning to Drive"	109-114
Mark Twain, "Uncle John's Farm"	155-162
N. Scott Momaday, "A Kiowa Grandmother"	172-179
Ralph Ellison, "Hidden Name and Complex Fate"	194-200
Judy Syfers, "I Want a Wife"	206-209
Joan Didion, "Marrying Absurd"	268-272
Lai Man Lee, "My Bracelet"	295-298
Andrew Hacker, "E.R.A.--R.I.P."	377-385
Jonathan Swift, "A Modest Proposal"	399-409
Angela Bowman, "Freddie the Fox and My Fifth Christmas"	470-474

7. **Education**

George Orwell, "Shooting an Elephant"	47-56
Tim Payne, "Bar Harbor, Maine"	75-79
Ann Upperco, "Learning to Drive"	109-114
Sheila Tobias, "Who's Afraid of Math, and Why"	122-129
James Thurber, "University Days"	231-238

Lai Man Lee, "My Bracelet"	295-298
Max Shulman, "Love Is a Fallacy"	409-422
Angela Bowman, "Freddie the Fox and My Fifth Christmas"	470-474

8. Social Issues

George Orwell, "Shooting an Elephant"	47-56
Frederick Douglass, "Resurrection"	57-63
Natalie Crouter, "Release from Captivity"	64-75
Jennifer McBride, "The Rock Fantasy"	142-147
Ralph Ellison, "Hidden Name and Complex Fate"	194-200
Judy Syfers, "I Want a Wife"	206-209
Laird Bloom, "The Progressives' Pilgrim"	221-224
Joan Didion, "Marrying Absurd"	268-272
Thomas Jefferson, "The Declaration of Independence"	340-345
Martin Luther King, Jr., "Letter from Birmingham Jail"	345-365
Frances FitzGerald, "Ethnic Bias in Textbooks"	365-377
Andrew Hacker, "E.R.A.--R.I.P"	377-385
George Orwell, "Marrakech"	388-399
Jonathan Swift, "A Modest Proposal"	399-409
Richard Rodriguez, "None of This Is Fair"	422-428

9. Responses to Crisis

George Orwell, "Shooting an Elephant"	47-56
Frederick Douglass, "Resurrection"	57-63
Natalie Crouter, "Release from Captivity"	64-75
Bill Bradley, "Fame and Self-Identity"	201-206
Thomas Jefferson, "The Declaration of Independence"	340-345
Martin Luther King, Jr., "Letter from Birmingham Jail"	345-365
Andrew Hacker, "E.R.A.--R.I.P"	377-385
George Orwell, "Marrakech"	388-399
Jonathan Swift, "A Modest Proposal"	399-409

10. The Arts

Rombauer, et al., "How to Cook Pasta"	85-90
Jennifer McBride, "The Rock Fantasy"	142-147
Laird Bloom, "The Progressives' Pilgrim"	221-224
Robert Brustein, "Reflections on Horror Movies"	250-261
Minoru Yamasaki, "The Aesthetics and Practice of Architecture"	281-289
James Agee, "Comedy's Greatest Era"	323-333

The Essay Connection: Readings for Writers

Index of Authors and Titles

(page numbers refer to pages in the text)

Aesthetics and Practice of Architecture, The, 281
Agee, James
  Comedy's Greatest Era, 323
Allen, Woody
  Selections from the Allen Notebooks, 13

Becker, Marion Rombauer
  Cooking Pastas, 85
Bloom, Laird
  The Progressives' Pilgrim: A Review of Lillian
    D. Wald's House on Henry Street, 220
Bowman, Angela
  Freddie the Fox and My Fifth Christmas: Past
    and Present, 470
Bradley, Bill
  Fame and Self-Identity, 201
Brown Wasps, The, 272
Brustein, Robert
  Reflections on Horror Movies, 250

Carson, Rachel
  Grey Beginnings, The, 97
Catton, Bruce
  Grant and Lee: A Study in Contrasts, 313
Comedy's Greatest Era, 323
Cooking Pastas, 85
Cosmic Calendar, The, 289
Crouter, Natalie
  Release from Captivity, 64

David, Elizabeth
  To Cook Spaghetti, 87
Declaration of Independence, The, 340
Didion, Joan
  Marrying Absurd, 268
  On Keeping a Notebook, 4
Dillard, Annie
  Transfiguration, 180
Douglass, Frederick
  Resurrection, 57

Eiseley, Loren
  Brown Wasps, The, 272
Elbow, Peter
  Freewriting, 18
Ellison, Ralph
  Hidden Name and Complex Fate, 194
E.R.A.--R.I.P, 377
Ethnic Bias in Textbooks, 365

Fame and Self-Identity, 201
FitzGerald, Frances
  Ethnic Bias in Textbooks, 365
Flower, Linda
  Writing for an Audience, 238
Freddie the Fox and My Fifth Christmas: Past and
    Present, 470
Freewriting, 18
From Egocentric Speech to Public Discourse: Richard
    Wright Composes His Thoughts on Black Boy, 445

Grant and Lee: A Study in Contrasts, 313
Grey Beginnings, The, 97

Hacker, Andrew
  E.R.A.--R.I.P., 377
Hazan, Marcella
  How to Cook Pasta, 87
Hidden Name and Complex Fate, 194
How to Cook Pasta, 87

I Want a Wife, 206
Interview Comments on Black Boy, 455

Jastrow, Robert
  Man of Wisdom, 136
Jefferson, Thomas
  Declaration of Independence, The, 340
John Fuller, Mail Carrier, 23
Jordan, Suzanne Britt
  That Lean and Hungry Look, 319

King, Kristin
  Ontonagon, 185
King, Jr., Martin Luther,
  Letter from Birmingham Jail, 345
Kiowa Grandmother, A, 172

Learning to Drive, 109
Lee, Lai Man
  My Bracelet, 295

Leonard, John
  Only Child, The, 28
Letter from Birmingham Jail, 345
Lopez, Barry
  My Horse, 305
Love Is a Fallacy, 409

Maker's Eye: Revising Your Own Manuscripts, The, 431
Man of Wisdom, 136
Marrakech, 391
Marrying Absurd, 268
McBride, Jennifer
  Rock Fantasy, The, 142
McPhee, John
  Pine Barrens, The, 163
Modest Proposal, A, 399
Momaday, N. Scott
  A Kiowa Grandmother, 172
Murray, Donald M.
  The Maker's Eye: Revising Your Own Manuscripts, 431
My Bracelet, 295
My Horse, 305

Neutral Spirit: A Portrait of Alcohol, The, 91
None of This Is Fair, 422

On Keeping a Notebook, 4
On Magic in Medicine, 130
On the Beach at Bar Harbor, 75
Once More to the Lake, 39
Only Child, The, 28
Ontonagon, 185
Orwell, George
  Marrakech, 391
  Shooting an Elephant, 47

Payne, Tim
  On the Beach at Bar Harbor, 75
Peterson, Linda
  From Egocentric Speech to Public Discourse: Richard Wright Composes His Thoughts on Black Boy, 445
Pine Barrens, The 163
Progressives' Pilgrim: A Review of Lillian D. Wald's The House on Henry Street, The, 220

Reflections on Horror Movies, 250
Release from Captivity, 64
Resurrection, 57

Rishta/Fresh Noodles, 86
Rock Fantasy, The, 142
Roden, Claudia
  Rishta/Fresh Noodles, 86
Rodriguez, Richard
  None of This Is Fair, 422
Rombauer, Irma S.
  Cooking Pastas, 85
Rouiché, Berton
  The Neutral Spirit: A Portrait of Alcohol, 91

Sagan, Carl
  The Cosmic Calendar, 289
Selections from the Allen Notebooks, 13
Shooting an Elephant, 47
Shulman, Max
  Love Is a Fallacy, 409
Style, 463
Swift, Jonathan
  A Modest Proposal, 399
Syfers, Judy
  I Want a Wife, 206

Technology of Medicine, The, 243
Terkel, Studs
  John Fuller, Mail Carrier, 23
That Lean and Hungry Look, 319
Thomas, Lewis
  On Magic in Medicine, 130
  The Technology of Medicine, 243
Thurber, James
  University Days, 231
To Cook Spaghetti, 87
Tobias, Sheila
  Who's Afraid of Math, and Why?, 122
Transfiguration, 180
Twain, Mark
  Uncle John's Farm, 155

Uncle John's Farm, 155
University Days, 231
Upperco, Ann
  Learning to Drive, 109

von Baeyer, Hans C.
  The Wonder of Gravity, 210

White, E.B.
  Once More to the Lake, 39
Who's Afraid of Math, and Why?, 122

Wonder of Gravity, The, 210
Wright, Richard
  Interview Comments on Black Boy, 455
Writing for an Audience, 238

Yamasaki, Minoru
  The Aesthetics and Practice of Architecture, 281

Zinsser, William
  Style, 463